Singing to the Goddess

Singing to the Goddess

Poems to Kālī and Umā from Bengal

Rachel Fell McDermott

OXFORD
UNIVERSITY PRESS
2001

OXFORD

Oxford New York
Athens Auckland Bangkok Bogotá Buenos Aires Calcutta
Cape Town Chennai Dar es Salaam Delhi Florence Hong Kong Istanbul
Karachi Kuala Lumpur Madrid Melbourne Mexico City Mumbai
Nairobi Paris São Paulo Shanghai Singapore Taipei Tokyo Toronto Warsaw

and associated companies in
Berlin Ibadan

Published by Oxford University Press, Inc.
198 Madison Avenue, New York, New York 10016

Library of Congress Cataloging-in-Publication Data
McDermott, Rachel Fell.
Singing to the goddess : poems to Kālī and Umā from Bengal /
Rachel Fell McDermott.
p. cm.
Includes index.
ISBN 0-19-513433-8—ISBN 0-19-513434-6 (pbk.)
1. Kālī (Hindu deity)—Poetry. 2. Parvati (Hindu deity)—Poetry.
3. Devotional poetry, Bengali—Translations into English. I. Title.
PK1714.5. E5 M337 2000
891.4'4104083829452114—dc21 99-088189

1 3 5 7 9 8 6 4 2

Printed in the United States of America
on acid-free paper

For
Narendra Nāth Bhaṭṭācāryya
and
Minati Kar

Śākta experts
mentors
friends

Acknowledgments

Singing to the Goddess: Poems to Kālī and Umā from Bengal derives its lifeblood from its much larger companion volume, *Mother of My Heart, Daughter of My Dreams: Kālī and Umā in the Devotional Poetry of Bengal* (New York: Oxford University Press, 2001). All of the Śākta poems excerpted and discussed in the latter book, plus many others, are presented in full here with minimal introductions so as to create an accessible anthology that can be used, especially for undergraduate courses but also for inspirational reading. Although all of the people whom I thanked in the larger book are in some ways responsible for this book as well, here I would like to single out those whose expertise has been particularly helpful to me in the arduous but ultimately delightful task of translation.

Institutionally, I am indebted to Harvard University—to Professors John B. Carman and Diana L. Eck, who supported and guided me in spite of the fact that poetry to Kālī is particularly relished by neither the Śrī Vaiṣṇava nor the north Indian Śaiva tradition—and to the university's Frank Knox Traveling Fellowship. Other funding that enabled me to live in Calcutta for two years and to complete my dissertation was provided by the Fulbright-Hays Doctoral Dissertation Research Abroad grant and the Institute of International Education Fulbright award, both administered in Calcutta by Dr. Umā Dāśgupta and the office of the United States Educational Foundation in India, and by the Charlotte W. Newcombe Fellowship. To all of these granting agencies I am most grateful. In the years since receiving the Ph.D., during which I decided to expand the project from a narrow emphasis upon the poetry of Kamalākānta Bhaṭṭācārya to include all of the poets in the 250-year literary tradition, I extend warm thanks to Barnard College for a travel stipend and to Professor Irene Bloom, chair of my department, who graciously allowed me to rush off to Calcutta for ten days each fall, partially to consult my Śākta poetry mentors during the Kālī Pūjā festivities. Most recently, the editors at Oxford University Press, especially Cynthia Read, Theodore Calderara, MaryBeth Branigan, and Nancy Hoagland deserve thanks for their shepherding of this book through the various stages of publication. Special gratitude goes to Margaret Case for her superb job of manuscript editing.

But let me return to the poetry itself. My interest began with my parents. I remember as a child at bedtime listening to my father read out passages from *The Gospel of Sri Ramakrishna*. These included Śākta poems sung to the saint by his disciples, which frequently sent him into an ecstatic mood. I always wanted my father to get through these poetry excerpts as fast as possible. To me they seemed full of flowery English and inscrutable meanings; I was far more interested in Ramakrishna's conversations and jokes. Rāmprasād and Kamalākānta, in other words, were household names, and I thank my parents, and Swami Nikhilananda's formal English translations, for introducing me to them at such a young age. Although my husband Scott views the Śākta poetry in a light similar to that of Rachel the child, he has selflessly supported me and this project, and much credit for its completion belongs to him.

In Calcutta, London, and New York, I have had several mentors and teachers, and the help of all of them stands behind and within the lines of poetry contained in this book. My Bengali teachers in Calcutta in 1988–1990, Keśabcandra Sarkār of the Ramakrishna Mission Institute of Culture and Aditi Sen of the American Institute of Indian Studies, read with me, helped familiarize me with the elliptical style of the eighteenth- to nineteenth-century Śākta poetry genre, and corrected my initial literal translations. Since 1993 I have also received help and advice, particularly in decoding language usages and images not found in any dictionary, by Henā Basu in Calcutta, Professor Partha Mitter in London, and Professors Jeffrey J. Kripal and Clinton B. Seely in the United States.

However, there are two scholars whose help towers above that of everyone else, whose guidance and willingness to review and correct my work have been foundational to whatever success these Bengali-to-English translations might hope to obtain. Professors Narendra Nāth Bhaṭṭācāryya of Calcutta University and Minati Kar of Viśvabhārati University are intellectual giants in the field of Śākta interpretation. From them I have learned as much about kindness as I have about the intricacies of Goddess-centered poetry conventions, and this book is gratefully and fondly dedicated to them.

Contents

Introduction

The Poems

Singing to the Goddess

Introduction

Pathways to the Śākta Poetry: Sources, Precedents, and Influences

The Bengali scholar Śaśibhūṣaṇ Dāśgupta, in commenting upon the Goddess-centered devotional poetry tradition of Bengal, once remarked that although it was not surprising to find Umā, the lovely wife of Śiva, softened and humanized by the touch of devotion, the effects of that touch upon Kālī were astonishing. Who would have thought that the black Goddess of death, who decapitates her enemies and hangs their body parts from her neck and around her waist, would become the embodiment of motherly compassion and kindness?[1]

In part because of the dread characteristics of this Goddess, bhakti, or devotion, came late to her literary tradition. Although we have evidence of bhakti poetry to male deities such as Viṣṇu and Śiva from as early as the ninth century in south India, and although love poetry to Kṛṣṇa flowered in Bengal from the fifteenth century on, it was not until the mid-eighteenth century that poets began addressing Kālī in the endearing language of intimacy. The resulting genre has been named Śākta Padāvalī, or Collected Poems to the Goddess, and is divided into two parts, both meant to be sung, usually to instrumental accompaniment. The first, Śyāmā-saṅgīta, or Songs to Śyāmā, the Black Goddess Kālī, has historically been the more popular, in terms of both composition and audience appeal. In these poems, the Goddess receives the full gamut of human emotion, for she is described, praised, blessed, petitioned, cajoled, and even threatened. The poets speak directly to Kālī, trying to get her attention and secure for themselves a place at her fear-dispelling feet. By contrast, Umā-saṅgīta, or Songs to Śiva's wife Pārvatī, tell a story. *Āgamanī* songs, or songs about her coming, celebrate Umā's once-yearly visit from her home with Śiva in Kailasa to her parents, Girirāj, the King of the Mountains, and his wife Menakā, somewhere in the Himalayas in northern Bengal. She arrives just at the commencement of the autumnal Durgā Pūjā festivities,[2] when the martial, ten-armed Durgā (with whom Umā is identified) is acclaimed for her killing of the buffalo demon Mahiṣa. She stays for the three days of the Pūjā and then returns home to her husband, much to the dismay of her parents and friends. *Vijayā* songs, or those sung on the last day, the day of victory (*vijayā*), when Durgā triumphs over the demon, lament Umā's incipient departure.

The Goddess as she appears in the poems of this genre has many faces, which reflect the several literary and historical phases of her Sanskrit and Bengali heritage.[3] Kālī or Kālikā as a name derives from *kāla*, which means "black," "time," and "death"; as such, she is the Mistress of Time or Death, the one who devours. Her history in the *Mahābhārata* epic and mythological stories of the Purāṇas from the early centuries C.E. attests to this characterization; she aids other gods and goddesses in their battles against demons, and is known for her blood-lust. The most famous Purāṇic text to feature Kālī is the sixth-century "Devī-Māhātmya" section of the *Mārkaṇḍeya Purāṇa*, where she is created by the Goddess Durgā or Caṇḍikā to help dispatch three particularly unruly demons, Caṇḍa, Muṇḍa, and Raktavīja. Although the main heroine of the text is Durgā in her victories over the buffalo demon Mahiṣa and the two demons Śumbha and Niśumbha, Kālī's successes and relationship to Durgā earn her a place in the growing pantheon of goddesses. She continues to appear in Purāṇas through the sixteenth century, where—despite her awe-inspiring, demon-chopping activities—she is increasingly described in philosophical language as a manifestation of Śakti, feminine potency, and as the highest Brahman, the absolute ground of being.

Through Kālī's identification with Durgā, and hence with Pārvatī or Umā, she also gains "the Auspicious Lord" Śiva as a husband; indeed, one of her most popular epithets in the Śākta poetry is Śaṅkarī, or Wife of Śaṅkara (Śiva). As such, Kālī is allied both to the Goddess Satī, daughter of Dakṣa, who committed suicide in reaction to her father's insult to her husband Śiva, and to Satī's reincarnated form in the person of Umā, Daughter of the Himalayas, who wins Śiva back through her asceticism and devotion. These stories about Satī and Umā derive at least from the time of the *Mahābhārata* and are amplified in subsequent Sanskrit plays and Purāṇas. As far as epic and Purāṇic texts are concerned, then, it is Umā and Durgā who are the most famous, the most written about. Kālī wins her acceptance in this literature through her association with them.

But already by the eleventh century, Kālī had gained another dimension through her incorporation into Tantric texts, rituals, and philosophical speculations. Tantra as a system of texts and ideas is esoteric, for the initiated few alone, and stands upon the principle that worldly things usually considered as obstacles to spiritual advancement need not be, if properly understood and handled. Hence Tantric texts offer complicated ritual and meditation prescriptions, detailed iconographic descriptions of deities to be worshiped, and instructions on the attainment of spiritual powers. In addition, they posit the human body as a microcosm of the spiritual universe: inside are to be found all elements of the material world, all pilgrimage sites, all deities, and the beginning and end of the religious path. Through one of the most celebrated Tantric spiritual practices, *kuṇḍalinī* yoga, the skilled aspirant learns to raise his spiritual energy, coiled as a female serpent (*kuṇḍalinī*) in the base of his spine, up through the six centers or *cakra*s in the central channel of his body (*mūlādhāra* at the base of the spine, *svādhiṣṭhāna* between the anus and penis, *maṇipura* at the navel, *anāhata* at the heart, *viśuddha* at the throat, and *ājñā* between the eyebrows).[4] His final destination is the seventh and last center, the *sahasrāra*, at the top of his head (see Fig. 1). There the *kuṇḍalinī* unites with her consort, Śiva, bringing to the aspirant the nondual liberation he has been seeking.

Bengali Śyāmā-saṅgīta is influenced by five aspects of this Tantric context: the conviction that one need not escape from the world in order to achieve full realization; the descriptions of Kālī's form, used for meditation; the hymns of praise for Kālī, which glorify her as the philosophical Absolute, the coincidence of opposites, and the font of compassion; the practice of *kuṇḍalinī* yoga, which many of the poets follow and exhort, and from which Kālī gains the epithet Kuṇḍalinī; and the name Tārā, the Savior, the One Who Takes (the devotee) Across (the sea of this world), one of Kālī's most common names. Tārā is an important goddess in Buddhist Tantra, and was probably absorbed into the Hindu pantheon and identified with Kālī sometime after the eleventh century.

Although Durgā in her various forms is to a lesser extent also described and worshiped in Tantric literature, Umā's place in this vast corpus is superficial. She is a stereotyped figure who, as Śiva's devoted wife, questions and elicits from him instructions about Tantric rites, philosophical ideas, and meditation procedures. Whereas Kālī comes to the Śākta poets imbued with a rich heritage of Tantric associations, Umā remains largely within a narrative provenance centered around her marriage and home life with Śiva.

Sanskrit texts are not the only foundation for the Kālī and Umā of Śākta Padāvalī. Bengali poetry since the medieval period has also made its impression. The genre of Maṅgalakāvya literature, long poems celebrating the exploits of various deities, preserves the evolving notions of the Goddess. Kālī does not become the subject of this genre until the seventeenth century, but when she does get incorporated—particularly in a story called "Vidyā-Sundara" from the *Kālikāmaṅgalakāvya*—she emerges as a slightly capricious but compassionate figure who acts to save her devotees from ignominy. Moreover, the frightening skulls, severed arms, and glistening blood that she wears on her body are beautified by the addition of jewels and tinkling bells, details later appropriated by the poets of the Śākta Padāvalī tradition. Umā's place in this genre is even more important, and forms a direct link with the *āgamanī* and *vijayā* poems. Several Maṅgalakāvyas, even if chiefly concerned to glorify another deity, also tell the story of Śiva and Pārvatī, but with particularly Bengali twists. Here Śiva is no handsome Lord but a good-for-nothing old man who has to till the land for a living, and who fritters away his money in drunken sprees. Umā is unhappy with him, and her parents grieve over their son-in-law.

The biggest Bengali influence upon the songs to Kālī, however, is the prior but parallel poetry tradition to Kṛṣṇa, Vaiṣṇava Padāvalī. The Śākta poets copied the form and style of the Vaiṣṇava poems, creating short, rhyming compositions that typically conclude with a *bhaṇitā*, or signature line, where the poet inserts his name and comments upon the subject of his poem. In terms of content, as well, the Vaiṣṇava tradition provided models: the grim Goddess Kālī is beautified with imagery very similar to that used for Kṛṣṇa's lover Rādhā (poem 19); Vaiṣṇava saints and pilgrimage sites are incorporated into the Śāktas' internal and external sacred geographies (poems 120 and 164); and the name of Kṛṣṇa—in the Bengali tradition usually Hari—is repeated reverentially in the context of devotion to the Goddess (poems 20 and 87). The influence is even more noticeable in the Umā-saṅgīta, where Menakā's yearning for, love of, and fears about her young daughter Umā remind one of Yaśodā's longing care for her foster-son Kṛṣṇa. Indeed, most Bengali scholars believe that the Śākta poets borrowed the Vaiṣṇavas' category of *vātsalya bhāva* (the feeling of a cow for her calf), which in the Vaiṣṇava setting is so well exemplified by Yaśodā's attitudes toward her son, and used it to express Menakā's love for Umā. Regarding Kālī, on the other hand, these scholars assert that the dominant emotion is *prati-vātsalya bhāva*, the love a child feels toward his or her mother.

Although the fact of this influence is not a matter of debate, the causes for it are. Was this incorporation of Vaiṣṇava elements a form of flattery, indicating that the regnant tradition of devotional poetry to Kṛṣṇa was so pervasive and beloved that any subsequent literary tradition had to follow in its steps? Perhaps. And yet there was also a sense of rivalry; in order for the newer Goddess cult to take hold, it had to present itself in a familiar garb, and yet argue for its ability to absorb and even supercede its predecessor. Hence the many Śākta poems that claim Kālī's identification with Kṛṣṇa (poems 24–27).

The final source for the conceptions and images found in the Śākta Padāvalī is neither the Sanskrit Purāṇic or Tantric literatures nor the Bengali genres of poetry, but local, oral sayings, linguistic forms, and attitudes toward the means of livelihood available in the mid-eighteenth to early nineteenth century. Particularly the earliest poets, Rāmprasād Sen and Kamalākānta Bhaṭṭācārya, fill their compositions with references to farmers and their debts; financial managers of landed estates; merchant traders and their capital ventures; lawyers in court battles; boatmen and their leaky vessels; poor people bewailing the inequities of class and wealth; and ordinary folk enjoying themselves in annual religious festivals and various amusements. When discussing their distressing lack of devotion, they often refer to the six sins—lust, anger, greed, lethargy, pride, and envy—in homey metaphors, as the six enemies, the six thieves, the six land-diggers, the six ingredients to be added to a spiritual stew, the six fires, and the six oarsmen. More recent poets continue this trend; Kalyāṇkumār Mukhopādhyāy, for example, describes receiving the Goddess's grace in terms of a modern train journey (poem 78). The same local touches are also evident in the Umā-saṅgīta, where the situations of Umā with Śiva and Menakā with Girirāj mirror those of married women in late-medieval to early-modern rural Bengal.

A brief look at the figure of Śiva—also called Śaṅkara and Hara, the Destroyer—reveals that he too is a multilayered individual. In many ways the Śiva one encounters here in the Śākta Padāvalī is the Purāṇic Śiva: the Lord of Kailasa, the ascetic married to Pārvatī, Daughter of the Mountain. But he is also a Tantric deity who, in the prescribed iconographic images of Kālī, lies beneath her feet as both corpse and sexual partner. Moreover, his greatness is proven by the fact that he is the only one who can fathom her, and it is he who is the ultimate goal of both the *kuṇḍalinī* and the poet-aspirant, who together rise to union with him in Tantric meditation. From such heights, the Śāktas' Śiva falls to moral and economic decrepitude in the Umā-saṅgīta, poems in direct continuity with the Bengali Maṅgalakāvyas. For here he is a mother-in-law's nightmare, who not only drags Umā into poverty but, in a manner reminiscent of the flirtatious Kṛṣṇa, womanizes on the side.

In addition to all of these aspects, none of which is discarded, the Śākta poets draw upon a late Purāṇic tradition that treats Śiva as Kālī's principal devotee.[5] Willingly becoming her "victim" so as to have her salvation-conferring feet on his chest, Śiva is the poets' father as well as their chief rival. For if they can snatch the feet away from him for themselves, they will have achieved the supreme object of their spiritual desire (poems 58, 65, and 71).

Poets for the Goddess

This anthology consists of 164 compositions by thirty-seven representative poets.[6] Although they span over 250 years, from the mid-eighteenth century to the present, as a group they have much in common. They are mostly men (only four are women); almost all of them are twice-born, from the upper three caste groupings in Bengal; the great majority lived or live in the regions now known as West Bengal; and with only one or two exceptions they can be classed as householders, not renouncers. However, since social and political conditions, as well as sources of patronage for artistic expression, have changed considerably over the last two and a half centuries in Bengal, there is quite a variation in the relationship among these poets, their writing of Śākta lyrics, and their means of livelihood. Indeed, although some of the poets chosen for this volume appear to have done little else but write devotional poetry to the Goddess, others wrote desultorily, on a number of topics; Śākta themes form a small, if interesting, part of their overall repertoires. Again, certain poets were fortunate to be patronized by men of wealth and social standing, whose support enabled them to give up regular quotidian work. Most of the more recent poets, by contrast, have had to nurture their artistic and religious proclivities as a hobby and publish poetry volumes on their own, or they have derived such little revenue from commercially produced work that they have had to take additional jobs. For the purposes of this anthology, therefore, "Śākta poet" does not necessarily indicate that the person in question was a Śākta—he could have been a litterateur, whose work says nothing about his personal religious orientation—or even that he wrote primarily on Śākta topics. Why such people have been included here has everything to do with their poetry, irrespective of personal motivation: if the poetry is important in the history of the evolving Śākta Padāvalī genre, it merits consideration.

The poets about whom biographic information is available can be divided into six very rough groups, the first three of which are contemporaries.[7]

1. Although it is extremely difficult to determine who initiated the genre of Śākta Padāvalī, it is clear who paid for it and who benefited from it: the zamindars, or owners of landed estates, most of whom lived in the western regions of Bengal.[8] By the mid-eighteenth century, a large number of such wealthy families had adopted Durgā and Kālī as their clan deities, and many scholars believe that the worship of such powerful, martial goddesses aided the zamindars in their quest for political and social prestige in a rapidly changing and unstable environment, where they had to negotiate between the rising of British ambitions and the threatened system of Mughal governance. The zamindars of Nadia, Burdwan, Dinajpur, and Rajshahi, the four biggest revenue-generating districts in Bengal, were all Śākta, patronized Śākta festivals, dabbled in the composition of Śākta lyrics, and maintained courts studded with poets, musicians, and philosophers—men whose learning and artistry reflected well on the sensibilities of their patrons. Sample poets from this category in the anthology include Śambhucandra Rāy and Naracandra Rāy, both of whom straddled the beginning of the nineteenth century and were born into the Nadia zamindari lineage; Mahārāja Rāmkṛṣṇa Rāy (d. 1795), zamindar of the Rajshahi estate in the east, who saw clear linkages between Goddess worship and temporal power (see poem 12); Mahārāja Nandakumār Rāy (d. 1775), a patron of the arts who grew in wealth and influence under the British in Calcutta and who was renowned as both a patron of and a believer in Śākta traditions; Mahārājādhirāja Māhtābcānd (1825–1879), zamindar of Burdwan and a prolific writer of Śākta bhakti poetry; and Āśutoṣ Deb (1805–1856), the doyen of an important Calcutta family, who sponsored religious, literary, and cultural events in the city, as well as writing his own poems, some on Śākta themes.

2. None of the estate owners appears to have written very much poetry, however; in the main they left this to the retainers in their employ. The *dewāns* or financial managers of several of the important aristocratic families also wrote Śākta poetry; famed Bengali examples are Dewān Raghunāth Rāy (d. 1836) of Burdwan, and Dewān Rāmdulāl Nandī (d. 1851) of Tripura. But by far the most important contributors to the entire 250-year tradition are two court poets who lived at the expense of the Nadia and Burdwan zamindars, respectively: Rāmprasād Sen (ca. 1718–1775) and Kamalākānta Bhaṭṭācārya (ca. 1769–1821). They appear to have had no other mandate than to compose poetry, although Kamalākānta also served as a priest in his patron's Kālī temple and tutored his patron's son. As a result, each one produced between two and three hundred Śākta poems. In addition, both are celebrated in Bengali history and legend as accomplished spiritual adepts, who combined a love of the Goddess with an expertise in Tantric practice.

3. A third group who sang on Śākta themes were professional entertainers of the mid-eighteenth to mid-nineteenth centuries who, like the poets in the second category above, were patronized by wealthy landowners inside and outside Calcutta. Unlike the *dewāns* and court poets mentioned above, however, they are not generally famed for their devotion or spirituality, although they may have had personal religious tendencies; rather, they are classed by Bengali commentators as performers

who made a living by going from one engagement to another, developing their repertoires and making a name for themselves. Usually singing in groups with orchestral accompaniment, these musicians specialized in extemporaneous composition, and often heightened the entertainment by performing with a rival group, whose wit and brilliance they attempted to outshine. Although, in terms of religious themes, such singers preferred to focus on the highly nuanced story of Rādhā and Kṛṣṇa, with its potential for social commentary on jilted love, they did occasionally sing about Umā and Śiva as well, emphasizing the sorrow of mother and daughter, or the plight of young girls. Kālī, less amenable of narrative treatment, is infrequently made the subject of their songs. And when she is, it is her association with Durgā and her epic and Purāṇic, not her Tantric, heritage that are typically plumbed (see poems 43, 58, and 102). The exception is Dāśarathi Rāy, who in addition to his longer poems on Umā and Śiva also composed a number of short poems on Kālī, Tantra, and devotion. Of these three have been excerpted here.

Because of the oral, spontaneous nature of these performances, and because they often occurred in the open, as street entertainment, much of this poetry has been lost. However, enough has been saved through the efforts of nineteenth-century anthologists to indicate how important their compositions were to the developing genre of Śākta poetry. Representative poets from this category include Raghunāth Dās (third quarter of the eighteenth century); Rām Basu (1738–1812); Nīlmaṇi Pāṭunī (d. 1825); Anthony Sāheb (d. 1836); Dāśarathi Rāy (1807–1857); Rasikcandra Rāy (1820–1893); Harināth Majumdār (1833–1896); Śāradā Bhāṇḍārī (n.d.); and Nabīncandra Cakrabartī (n.d.).

4. After the mid-nineteenth century, sources of patronage change. With the more aggressive Anglicizing programs of the British, the growing cleavage between English-educated, "polite" society and the folk culture of the streets, and the development of Bengali prose and drama often patterned on or in opposition to British models, a number of professional litterateurs emerged. These were men whose success was judged by the publication or public staging of their work, rather than its performance in the parlors of the rich. Again, such artists wrote on a number of varied themes, and Śākta topics assumed only a fraction of their total output. Nevertheless, because they were accomplished writers, their poetry is interesting. Examples chosen for this volume include the poet Nīlkaṇṭha Mukhopādhyāy (1841–1912), the journalist and anthologist Īśvarcandra Gupta (1818–1859), and the playwright Giriścandra Ghoṣ (1844–1912). Ghoṣ, in particular, was an admirer of the Śākta saint, Rāmkṛṣṇa (1836–1886), the most famous Kālī devotee of his time.

5. One of the most intriguing, if short-lived, uses of the Kālī and Umā material was during the early decades of the twentieth century, when nationalists called for Bengalis to conceive of their motherland as a goddess. Although this goddess was rarely named Kālī, Durgā, or Umā—typically she was simply Mā (Mother) or Bhārata Mātā (Mother India)—she certainly took over their functions: like Kālī, the Mother of the World, her help was sought in reducing prejudice between her children; like the ten-armed Durgā, she was called upon to use her martial powers

to rid India of foreigners; and like Umā, she was importuned not to leave on Vijayā until she had cleansed Bengal of (white) demons; see poems 89, 155, 156, 163, and 164, by Mahendranāth Bhaṭṭācārya (1843–1908) and Najrul Islām (1899–1976), the only Muslim to contribute to this literary genre. Although, as a whole, there are remarkably few references in the entire Śākta poetry to contemporary events, these politicized poems demonstrate that Bengali goddesses have been, and could again be, inspirational in galvanizing patriotic fervor.

Mahendranāth and Najrul are also the first two poets after Rāmprasād and Kamalākānta to write a significant number of poems on Śākta themes; because of this, and the excellent quality of their compositions, they may be considered as the first truly important literary heirs of the early poets. Further, Mahendranāth, like Rāmprasād and Kamalākānta before him, was famed as a holy man, someone whose poetry flowed from hours of meditation on Kālī.

6. Finally, we turn to poets who have been writing since the 1970s, some of whom have published their songs in books (Āśutoṣ Bhaṭṭācārya, Dīnrām, Bhadreśvar Maṇḍal, Kalyāṇkumār Mukhopādhyāy, Rāmreṇu Mukhopādhyāy, and Gaṇapati Pāṭhak), and others who have come to public recognition principally through cassette and compact disc recordings (Mā Bāsantī Cakrabarttī, Śyāmāpad Basu Rāy, and Tāpas Rāy). Three of the four authors about whom I have been able to gather information—Dīnrām, Bhadreśvar Maṇḍal, and Gaṇapati Pāṭhak[9]—worked all their lives in government service, education, and banking, respectively; lacking a patron such as might have been available in the eighteenth century, their poetry writing has been perforce a hobby, though it reflects real love for the Goddess. Of the nine composers, Dīnrām and Mā Bāsantī Cakrabarttī are in many ways the most interesting from a literary standpoint. Dīnrām, a pseudonym, is one of few modern poets to write on Tantric *kuṇḍalinī* yoga, and Mā Bāsantī Cakrabarttī, the celibate head of her own ashram in Calcutta and one of the only women in the entire Śākta Padāvalī corpus, expresses in her lyrics the concerns of a Bengali housewife, who prefers the domestic situation of Pārvatī and Śiva to the unbecoming dominance of Śiva by Kālī (poems 30 and 53).

In sum, although the early poets Rāmprasād and Kamalākānta are deservedly the most popular among Śākta Padāvalī enthusiasts, not only as poets but also as men of great devotion, the tradition initiated by them has grown and expanded over the past two centuries and has produced several poets of great creativity. Just as it is clear with respect to image, language, and emotional timbre that Kamalākānta copied Rāmprasād, however, so also subsequent poets copied both Rāmprasād and Kamalākānta. As a result, much of what has been and continues to be published is derivative, with metaphors and phrases from the early poets reappearing years later in less accomplished form. This is certainly not a problem within a devotional framework; after all, does the Goddess care about poetic brilliance? But from a literary critical standpoint, one must say that with a few exceptions, notably Najrul Islām, Mahendranāth Bhaṭṭācārya, and perhaps Dīnrām—men who wrote voluminously, with sensitivity and novelty—the genre has remained firmly anchored in the path charted by its progenitors.

Family Resemblances: Śākta Padāvalī as Bhakti Poetry

There is much in the Śyāmā-saṅgīta and Umā-saṅgīta that reminds one of bhakti poetry in other centuries and sites in India. Attitudes toward the divine are emotive, highly personal, pervaded with an undercurrent of love and adoration, and expressed in an earthy vernacular that abounds with regional words and metaphors; grace and self-surrender are emphasized; the teacher's guidance is frequently alluded to; the philosophical language of absolutes, superlatives, and coincidences of opposites is called upon to substantiate claims about the Goddess's preeminence; and, like much devotional poetry elsewhere, the Śākta songs give few hints about the actual historical circumstances of their authors' lives.[10]

But there are also a number of peculiarities in this poetry tradition, characteristics that appear to separate the Bengali genre from, say, the Tamil or the Hindi. First, as a community of mainly upper-caste poets, they almost never denigrate caste boundaries; intriguingly, the only one to do so is Najrul Islām, a Muslim (poems 155 and 156). Second, although many of the professional entertainers may have traveled widely, and although bards may have carried the most popular compositions of their contemporaries from place to place in Bengal, there is no tradition of wandering per se; the legends of the famed poets are replete with examples of their planning, and then canceling, trips to celebrated pilgrimage places, claiming in song that all necessary holy spots are at the Goddess's feet (poems 93–95). Third, although this Bengal-centered emphasis might lead one to suspect that the poems would be full of references to specific Bengali sites, temples, or images of the Goddess, such is not the case. Save for the modern period, when poets like Śyāmāpad Basu Rāy praise Kālī and the Daksinesvar Temple, home to her saints Rāmkṛṣṇa and Śāradā Debī (poem 88), there is absolutely nothing parallel to "my lord of the meeting rivers" or "my lord white as jasmine" of the Tamil Śaivite bhakti poetry tradition.[11] Fourth, because the chief deities to whom most devotional poetry has been written—Śiva, Viṣṇu, and Kṛṣṇa—are male, and because there is an established custom of male poets identifying with a female figure in order to experience the height of union with the deity, God in these other traditions can be conceived as the poet's Beloved. Such is rarely the case for the Bengali poets, since it is taboo to imagine having a lover-beloved relationship with one's Mother. As mentioned above, *vātsalya* and *prati-vātsalya* are the type of intimacy typically enjoyed in the Śākta poetry. The one exception is, of course, Tantra, where the adept is encouraged either to watch the lovemaking of Śiva and Śakti in the *sahasrāra* at the top of his head (poems 7–9 and 106), or to identify with the *kuṇḍalinī* in her journey to and then union with Śiva (poems 104–105). The only place where the poet is told to imagine himself, as Śiva, having sex with the Goddess is in the context of the five-"m" ritual, the mechanics of which the poets never discuss.[12]

There are two further important distinctions between the Bengali devotional poetry and that of other vernaculars. Here there are no lines of succession between one poet and another, no clear evidence that poets knew each other or studied with each other, and no one from within the poetry tradition itself who wrote a spiritual history of the movement. We know from the similarities between poems that the poets must have heard each other's compositions, but how remains a mystery. Even to this day, there are very few singing groups devoted to the perpetuation of the genre. One locally famous exception is the Āndul Kālī-Kīrtan Samiti, a band of men, all Kālī-worshiping householders, who carry on the tradition of singing Mahendranāth Bhaṭṭācārya's compositions in temples and religious functions. In addition, there are several famed artists who commercially record the songs of Rāmprasād, Kamalākānta, and others, but their milieu is the concert hall, and they treat Śākta Padāvalī more as a cultural heritage than as the means to spiritual advancement.

Finally, although bhakti is certainly the underlying flavor of most of the poems in this anthology, it is by no means predominant in all. As the samples in the section on "Prioritizing Paths" (p. 93–102) attest, sometimes Tantric meditation is juxtaposed with devotion, and is said to be superior. Indeed, although most poems of the mid-nineteenth century and after are squarely dualistic, in which the aspirant aims to love, not merge with, the Goddess, the same is not true for the earliest poems by Rāmprasād and Kamalākānta who, more thoroughly Tantric in orientation, desire to become one with the divine.

The Challenges and Choices in Designing an Anthology

The most popular anthology of Śākta songs in Bengali is *Śākta Padābalī*, edited by Amarendranāth Rāy and published by the Calcutta University in 1942. This book has remained continuously in print since that date (though never updated), and is used as a text in courses on Bengali literature at the Calcutta University. If a university library in the United States has any Bengali collection of Śākta songs, it is likely to be Rāy's, and I have seen well-thumbed copies of the book beside the harmoniums of professional Bengali singers in Calcutta, to be mined for recordable songs.[13]

Śākta Padābalī contains 335 songs by 114 composers and is divided thematically into sixteen sections, without individual introductions. Although *Singing to the Goddess* is far from being a translation of Rāy's work,[14] in the planning and design of my anthology I have been greatly influenced by his, especially because of its importance in Bengali higher education over the last sixty years. However, in four ways the present volume differs from the model established by the Bengali precedent.

The great benefit of Rāy's collection is its breadth and scope, particularly for the eighteenth to nineteenth centuries; he has included poems by all known zamindars, *dewāns*, street entertainers, litterateurs, and dramatists, even if they wrote only one or two Goddess-centered lyrics their whole lives. He also deliberately juxtaposed poems of similar content or language to show continuities and borrowing.

In a smaller anthology, one has neither of these luxuries. My guiding principle has been to cover all the traditional topics with as wide a range of poets as possible, but, in the event of having to choose between two poems on the same theme, to translate the poem that is better written and has more interesting, perhaps novel, imagery. Hence, whereas a truly representative anthology would include the one extant poem by Mahārāja Kṛṣṇacandra Rāy, Rāmprasād's patron and one of the most important sponsors of Śākta ritual in mid-eighteenth-century Bengal, it does not appear here because it mirrors sentiments expressed better by Rāmprasād. Indeed, there is much in this literary tradition that is repetitive; this may be fine for the devotee, who reads the poems for spiritual uplift, but not for the general reader. In thus favoring novelty and literary quality as criteria for selection, I am departing from the tradition, which values instead the virtue of continuity and the pure evocation of religious sentiment. However, all seventeen composers whom Rāy quotes most often find a place in this anthology as well, even if I have chosen poems different from the ones he did to represent their talent.[15] The only exception I make to my own rule concerns female poets, whose voices, even up to the present, are so few that I have tried wherever possible to incorporate them, even if the poetry is not of the highest standard.[16]

A second choice has concerned how to give adequate voice to Bengali audience sentiment. Many of the Śākta songs have been popularized through records, cassettes, or compact discs; some, in fact, have been continuously recorded and re-recorded from the 1930s to the present. *Singing to the Goddess* is not a *Biggest Hits of . . .* volume, but one does want to be sensitive to Bengali opinion. As far as possible, I have tried, in considering poems for inclusion, to choose those that are also beloved by the public, so that if a Bengali were to pick up this volume and look through the index of first lines for her favorite lyrics, she would find them translated. However, if a poem in question appears to be popular principally because of its tune, or if its lyrics are not particularly noteworthy, I have passed it over in favor of another that is better expressed or, for instance, carries the Umā-Menakā story line in a new direction, even if it has never been lifted out of an anthology for studio recording. Where appropriate, the notes at the end of this volume indicate which poems have been recorded and where, and there is a discography for those interested in listening to a much wider range of Śākta Padāvalī.

Third, the present anthology updates Rāy's collection, both by adding composers writing in the genre since the 1940s and by reaching back into the past to include poets who did not make it into his list of authors. The most important in the latter category is the Muslim poet Najrul Islām, who is one of the most innovative composers in the genre since Rāmprasād Sen. Two others are Śāradā Bhāṇḍārī and Tāriṇī Debī, women about whom almost nothing is known but who, together with Andha Caṇḍī and Mā Bāsantī Cakrabarttī, the modern lyricist, are four of the few women writers in the entire Śākta Padāvalī corpus.

Fourth, a word about content. A comparison between *Śākta Padābalī* and *Singing to the Goddess* will reveal that some of the traditional topics are treated differently in the two volumes. Relatively speaking, poems on the themes of battle, advice to the mind, and death receive equal weight in both anthologies. However, Rāy chose to emphasize petitionary poems to Kālī and the *āgamanī* and *vijayā* poems to Umā far more than I have, whereas I have included more poems of complaint and an entire section on Tantric *kuṇḍalinī* yoga, which he completely omitted. This last point is significant: in almost all Bengali anthologies that do not present the whole of a poet's work—say, selections of Rāmprasād or Kamalākānta—the poems left out are those with Tantric import and those that depict Śiva and Kālī in union in the *sahasrāra*. Such poems are considered too esoteric or too scandalous for a general audience. They are nevertheless a genuine part of the genre and deserve a place in its English representation.

To conclude, a note about the history of Śākta Padāvalī in English translation. It was Mahendranāth Gupta, the disciple and biographer of Rāmkṛṣṇa, who first introduced the Śākta songs to an English audience with his translation of the *Kathāmṛta* in 1907.[17] Rāmprasād, Kamalākānta, and a host of other poets, Śākta as well as Vaiṣṇava, were favorites of Rāmkṛṣṇa, and he and his disciples would sing them together, sending the saint into spiritual ecstasy. Since they were threaded into a narrative about Rāmkṛṣṇa's sayings and activities, however, the songs were not always quoted in their entirety and often lacked any indication as to author. The first real anthology was compiled by Edward Thompson and Arthur Spencer, whose *Bengali Religious Lyrics, Śākta*, complete with introduction and biographical notes on the poets, was published in 1923.[18] This remained the only collection of Goddess-centered Bengali devotional poetry available outside the Bengali-speaking world until Jadunath Sinha and Michèle Lupsa published their English and French versions of Rāmprasād's poetry in 1966 and 1967.[19] In 1994, Lex Hixon updated the language of Sinha's translations in his *Mother of the Universe: Visions of the Goddess and Tantric Hymns of Enlightenment*,[20] but as he did not work from the Bengali and only reconfigured Sinha's English, this is not a reliable set of translations. The best collection of Rāmprasād's poetry to appear in English is *Grace and Mercy in Her Wild Hair: Poems to the Mother Goddess*, translated by Leonard Nathan and Clinton Seely in 1982.[21] These poems are so beautifully rendered that they set a standard for translation in the genre.[22]

Notes on Transliteration, Translation, and Word Definition

To enable better comprehension for readers unfamiliar with Bengali, I have used standard Sanskrit transliteration conventions to render all terms, names of deities, and types of textual genres. However, names and nicknames of Bengali poets, authors, and singing groups, as well as the texts or anthologies they authored, are written with Bengali conventions. The same is true for first lines of poetry cited in notes, and for any terms that do not have exact Sanskrit equivalents (such as the Caḍak or Gājan festival, the police chief *koṭāl*, and the name Ṭhākur to refer to a chosen deity). Although the Mughal term for financial steward is written as *deoyān* in Bengali, I have followed the lead of many historians in transliterating it as *dewān* or, when part of a person's title, Dewān. The names of geographic sites, towns, rivers, and temples are all rendered without diacritics and, where available, in recognized Anglicized forms. Words that have entered the English language are not italicized and are printed without diacritics.

In keeping with the ambiance of the Umā-centered poems, the majority of which are spoken by Umā's mother, who does not see her daughter as the Goddess, I have not capitalized personal pronouns that refer to Umā.

Since Mā is so pervasive in this poetry genre, to refer either to Kālī as "Mother" or to Umā as "little mother" in an affectionate form of address to a small girl, I have often left it as is in the English translations.

Whenever a Bengali epithet or term appears for the first time in the text, it is defined there, or in the note to the appropriate poem, and then not in subsequent usages. For the convenience of the reader, the most common such words are defined in the glossary, "A Guide to Selected Names, Terms, and Text," on page 173.

The Poems

Kālī among the Corpses: Poems of Battle

We begin with Kālī in her fiercest and perhaps oldest guise. These battlefield poems—together with those on the *kuṇḍalinī*, translated near the end of the anthology—reflect more than any other type of poem the Tantric origins of the Śākta literary tradition, and hence reach back into medieval conceptions of the Goddess's character. All of the poems to follow are modeled on the Tantric *dhyānas*, or descriptions of a deity used as an aid to the mental construction and installation of her in the heart, for the purpose of meditation. Below is a literal translation of the most famous of these for Kālī, as an example of the Sanskrit prototype from which the Bengali battlefield poetry is taken.

> Terrible-faced, horrible, with disheveled hair and four arms,
> Divine, adorned with a necklace of sliced-off heads;
> Holding in Her two left hands a freshly hacked head and a cleaver,
> And in Her right displaying the "fear not" and boon-bestowing hand gestures;
> Lustrously black like a large cloud, and robed with nothing but the sky,
> Anointed with blood dripping down from the necklace of heads at Her throat;
> Terrible because of the pair of children's corpses She wears for earrings,
> Her teeth horrid and Her face frightful, but Her breasts high and uplifted;
> A skirt of cut arms hanging from Her waist, laughter bellowing out,
> Her face shining from the red stream dripping from the two corners of Her mouth;
> Shouting terribly, dwelling on the very fierce cremation grounds,
> Her third eye permeated with the newly risen sun;
> With fangs for teeth and a pearl necklace that swings to the right as She moves,
> Sitting on the Great Lord, who has taken the form of a corpse;
> Surrounded by jackals and their terrible, all-pervading cries,
> Engaging Great Time in the act of reversed sexual intercourse;
> Her face happy and pleased, like a lotus—
> He who thinks on Kālī thus will have all his wishes fulfilled.[23]

Other Kālī-*dhyānas* add that she is accompanied by her ghoulish friends and that she has a half-moon on her forehead; the sun, moon, and fire for her three eyes;

matted hair; a lolling tongue thirsting for wine or the blood of corpses; a snake draped around her as a sacred thread; and a body black as mascara, adorned with all manner of jewels and ornaments. She is so brilliant that even the gods worship her.

In all of the available Tantric descriptions of this Goddess, the macabre is combined with the soothing, the fearsome with the pacific, so as to create a purposeful tension (see Fig. 2). The Bengali poets are true to this aspect of the Sanskrit literary tradition and draw upon the same imagery. A few, in fact, do no more than to render the *dhyānas* into Bengali. This is especially true of the early zamindars, who self-consciously undertook a program of popularizing Tantric texts, deities, and rites through translations into the vernacular. Poem 1, by Kamalākānta's patron's son, Mahārājādhirāja Māhtābcānd, is an example, notable for its clear reliance on the Sanskrit *dhyāna* given above. However, most Bengali Śākta poets depart from the Tantric model in four principal ways. First, they add movement to the picture, transforming the Tantric icon—static, intended for meditation—into a dynamic scene. Often evocative of the Purāṇic "Devī-Māhātmya" story, the Bengali setting is less a cremation ground than a battlefield, in which Kālī is worsting her demon enemies (in particular, Caṇḍa, Muṇḍa, and Raktavīja). Much more attention is devoted to her mastication of her foes than in the Sanskrit *dhyānas*. In addition, she is stomping, dancing, and creating havoc, rather than simply standing or sitting on Śiva. In other words, the Tantric descriptions have been colored by Purāṇic narrative elements.

Second, the Bengali poets beautify and humanize Kālī more than their Sanskrit literary predecessors. They do this by borrowing from classical descriptions of feminine beauty in order to depict the Goddess's youth, her navel, breasts, and thighs; by comparing aspects of her appearance with natural phenomena, such as flowers, birds, or rivers; by adding ornaments, such as tinkling bells, to parts of her blood-covered body (poem 3); and by depicting the love between Kālī and Śiva in explicit language, where reversed sexual intercourse is not simply stated, as in the *dhyānas*, but depicted (poems 7, 8, and 9), and where the language and imagery used to illustrate their love is reminiscent of that between Rādhā and Kṛṣṇa. Note that in poems 18, 19, and 20 the scene is less and less recognizably either the cremation or the battle ground; Kālī's traditional iconographic elements have almost disappeared, in favor of classical and Vaiṣṇava images. A Vaiṣṇava song is even sung in the context of her worship in poem 20. Although most poets follow this sweetening trend, begun in the Tantras and given new impetus by Rāmprasād, not all do. Poem 10, by Dāśarathi Rāy, shows how the Goddess appears when there is almost nothing to mitigate her fierce nature.

The addition of *bhaṇitās* is a third departure from the Tantric template, permitting the poets to personalize the *dhyānas* so that their compositions are less instruction for meditation than opportunities to talk to the Goddess directly or to convey the poets' states of mind. They express a range of emotions in such signature lines: devotion, petition, horror, triumph, and engrossed amazement, as well as sarcastic censure. For the disjunction between Kālī the dread demon slayer and Kālī the beautiful picture of modesty is a cause for bewilderment and an occasion for the poets to accost their Goddess, sometimes playfully, sometimes with more bite. Who is *this*? How can Kālī be a girl from a respectable family—indeed, a gentlewoman—when she acts so dishonorably? The sense of real or mock shame at the Goddess's appearance and behavior is an indication that the Bengali poets are dealing inventively with a difficult, or at the very least, complex, inherited deity.

Finally, after personalizing Kālī and creating a literary space for themselves in relation to her, the Bengali poets also turn their attention to Śiva or Hara. He remains the corpse beneath Kālī's feet, to be sure. But he is also her sexual partner, the victim of her mad stomping, on whose behalf Kamalākānta pleads to the Goddess in poem 15, and her chief devotee. He too, in other words, has been drawn into the narrative of devotion.

Over the past two centuries, fewer and fewer Śākta poets have chosen to write on this Tantric battlefield theme. This has been for two reasons: knowledge about and involvement with Tantra has lessened among authors writing in the genre; and the Goddess herself has become increasingly identified with a loving mother, whom one would not like to describe in gory or sexual terms. The seeds for such a development are contained already in Rāmprasād's corpus. Compare, for instance, poems 6 and 17. In the former, collected in 1862, Śiva is a corpse, and Kālī is clearly dominant over him. The latter, on the other hand, printed for the first time in the 1890s and almost certainly not original to the earliest Rāmprasād, presents a picture of a demure wife who would never step on her husband. It is as if the shame at Kālī's iconography and wild nature—expressed boldly or in jest by the early poets—has become real, and a cause for respectful silence.

1

Who is this, all alone? Whose woman is She,
shining like the moon, inky black? She's dread of face,
with blood streaming from Her mouth
and from Her tongue
clamped between Her teeth—yet She's young
and the flying streams of hair on that terrible body
shine. A pearl necklace swings at Her throat,
a girdle of human hands encircles Her waist.
Her breasts, plump and jutting out,
and the rest of Her monstrous body
are covered with rivers of blood. I see Her
children's corpses at Her ears, a half-moon on Her forehead, naked.
This woman plays on the battlefield, Her left hands holding a sword and a head,

and Her right signaling "fear not!" and boons.
Her clothes are horrifying, and so is She, standing on Bhava's chest
with Her right foot forward. In every direction on the cremation grounds
the jackals howl and Śaṅkarī cackles horridly.

Candra says: Promise me
that at my end I can meditate on You like this
Oh three-eyed Kālī.

Mahārājādhirāja Māhtābcānd

2

What a joke!
She's a young woman
from a good family
yes, but
She's naked—and flirts, hips cocked
when She stands.

With messy hair
roars awful and grim
this gentlewoman tramples demons
in a corpse-strewn battle.
But the God of Love
looks and swoons.

While ghosts, ghouls, and goblins
from Śiva's retinue, and Her own companions
nude just like Her
dance and frolic on the field,
She swallows elephants
chariots, and charioteers
striking terror into the hearts
of gods, demons, and men.

She walks fast,
enjoying Herself tremendously.
Human arms hang from Her waist.

Rāmprasād says: Mother Kālikā,
preserver of the world,
have mercy!
Take the burden:

ferry me across this ocean of becoming.
Hara's woman,
destroy my sorrows.

Rāmprasād Sen

3

Hey! Who is She, dark as clouds,
nubile, naked, shameless,
captivating hearts? Most improper
for a family girl!
Stomping like an elephant,
dizzy with drink, tongue
distended, hair
flying, crushing demons
horrid shrieks—
what a sight!
Men and gods recoil in fear.

Who is She? Her fingers
blossoming blue lotus buds
bitten by bees, Her face
the full moon—
So think the *cakora* birds
offering themselves at Her lips.
A dispute begins: is She
the bees' blue lotus
or the *cakoras*' moon?
"Chi-chi" chirp the birds,
"Gun-gun" drone the bees.

Who is She?
Her loins are exquisite, and Her thighs
streaming with blood
bring to mind
sturdy banana plant stalks.
Above them around Her waist
She has threaded human hands on a string, adding
tinkling bells for decoration.
With the fairest of hands
She grasps a sword and severed head on the left,
and promises boons and protection on the right.

While She hacks to pieces
horses, chariots, elephants
Her companions cheer Her on—
"Victory! Victory!"

Who is She?
Demons see Her breasts
very lofty mountains
and strike their elephants' heads
in fear
to get away.
What could be more amazing?
The Beautiful One beautifies Herself
with heads
Caṇḍa's and Muṇḍa's! strung
on a necklace!

The sweetest smile breaks out on Her cheerful face;
in a dazzling flash of teeth, lightning shoots
to sparkle in Her nose jewel.
With a wink of Her eyes
sun, fire, and moon
She stomps
up
and down
and the earth
quakes
and quakes.

Rāmprasād Sen

4

Who is this
delighting in war
dancing naked with witches
on the battlefield?
The rays of the morning sun
and ten moons
glisten in Her toenails.

Amazing! Her body
black as clouds

pierces darkness with its sheen,
and Hara, a cadaver,
is fallen at Her feet.

There too lie
brilliant reds and whites, intoxicating
javā and *bilva* flowers,
heaped by the immortals.

She's got hair blacker than clouds, eyes shot
with the lotus's red, a distended, dangling tongue,
and a face
a horrible face
with streams of blood
oozing from Her lips.
The earth trembles at Her arrogance.

Suddenly a dreadful shriek,
a blast of fire—lightning explodes from Her eyes
to dance playfully
in the sparkle of Her teeth.

This is a frightful sight; it can make you fear.
But for a devotee
She's a blessing who takes away fear.
Her Lowly One says: This is no ordinary being
but the risen form
of the Goddess Whose Essence Is Brahman.

Raghunāth Rāy

5

Who is this enchantress
lighting up the war field
by Her black beauty?
Whose woman
with huge eyes
and a dreadful face
adorns Herself for battle
with a garland of heads?

Jackals are dancing
among the corpses and noncorpses,
making horrid noises. Joining them

She cackles aloud
a hideous laughter
and places Her feet
on the heart of corpse-like Śiva,
tousling Her long
thick hair.

Kamalākānta stares
absorbed
not even blinking his eyes.

Kamalākānta Bhaṭṭācārya

6

Her face
is a spotless moon
ever blissful
drinking nectar,
Her body
graceful, startling the bodiless God of Love.
Oh King, don't be shocked
but Śiva
whom you take as Brahman
is a corpse
at Her feet!

Who is this woman on the battlefield?
She wears a sliver of the moon,
embodies all virtues
and smiles sweetly
Honey Lips!
This is hard for a man to bear.

Think of it:
She illumines the earth, Her three eyes
moon, sun, and fire
flashing light.

This sweetheart is the best of all
and of course
virtuous but

whose daughter is She
and what has She come searching for on the battlefield?

Look at Her deformed companions:
their nails
bowed bamboo winnowing baskets
their radish teeth, rumpled hair, and dusty bodies
scare me.

Poet Rāmprasād says,
Shield Your slave
who cries out
"Mā!"
in utter horror.
If You don't forgive his sins
Śyāmā, Umā
who will call You "Mother"?

Rāmprasād Sen

7

Unperturbed at the battle,
frightful ghouls dance
saying "Victory to Kālī! Kālī!"
Śaṅkarī, immersed in the waves of battle,
feels the spring breezes pleasant.

That very Brahmā, Lord of the Earth,
whose wives smear red powder on His blessed body,
when in the form of Śyāmā
plays with blood-red colors
in the company of Her female attendants.

Sweating with the fun
of reversed sexual intercourse,
young Śyāmā's flesh thrills
on top of young Śiva,
Her boat
amidst the deep ocean of nectar.
Her long hair reaches down to the ground.
She is naked,
ornamented with human heads and hands.

Kamalākānta watches their beautiful bodies
and sheds tears of bliss.

Kamalākānta Bhaṭṭācārya

8

So, forgetful Mahādeva,
You have fallen in love!

You got Her footprints
and now there's no separating You;
staring, staring,
You worship Her.
Her heavy locks of hair,
darker than a mass of clouds,
fall disheveled over Her body.
Incomparably glamorous!
Who knows the greatness of either of You—
You sky-clad sixteen-year-old,
and You, naked Tripurāri?

There is no end
to the bliss of Madana's Bewitcher.
Lying lazily under the woman's hold,
He thirsts for the taste of love play.
Saying endearing things
He makes love to the beautiful one
in the lotus heart of Kamalākānta.

Kamalākānta Bhaṭṭācārya

9

There's a huge hullabaloo in my lotus heart;
my crazy mind is getting me in trouble again!

It's a carnival for crazies—
two madcaps copulating!
Again and again
the Bliss-Filled Goddess collapses

in ecstacy
on the Lord Ever-Blissful.
I stare at this, speechless;
even the senses and six enemies are silent.
Taking advantage of this confusion,
the door of knowledge opens.

Crazy Premik says,
Everyone tells me I'm muddle-headed,
but can the son of confirmed crackpots
be normal?

Listen Mā Tārā, Remover of the World's Sins,
I'm going to cherish this moment;
and when at the end
I'm submerged in the water
take Your son onto Your lap.

Mahendranāth Bhaṭṭācārya

10

Who is this black
drunk female elephant?
She dances naked on the battlefield, tongue
    distended
        teeth bared.
            Her black form lights the three worlds.
With a head in one hand,
more heads beaded on a necklace
and corpses at Her ears,
She delights in two recent additions
    Caṇḍa's and Muṇḍa's heads
        then drinks the blood of Raktavīja.

The woman's hair
falls to the earth, Her crown
reaches the sky. Yawning open
    a gaping mouth
        She devours demons in droves.

Wearing a half-moon, bearing a sword,
    She jumps stomps bumps thumps
on the earth, who trembles

under Her weight. That's why the Ganges-Holder
took Her feet
and stood them on His chest.

Demons see Her awful appearance
Her four hands
and flee away. "How can we calm Her down?
How to escape?"

Four-handedly She destroys
horses and elephants, their blood
gushing out in rivers. Jackals
as well as Her other friends
demons, witches, and fiends
swim in those waves.

Blood everywhere
all Her limbs and body parts:
How to describe its sheen?
a red *javā* flower
floating on billowy black waters
in the Kalindi River.

Rumbling like a deep cloud of destruction
aiming like a pouncing lion
for the stag,
Her blood-shot eyes tell all.
Dāśarathi's Enemy
kills and laughs.

Dāśarathi Rāy

11

The World-Mother's police chief
goes strolling
in the dead of night.
"Victory to Kālī! Victory to Kālī!" he shouts
clapping his hands
and "bab bam!"
striking his cheeks.

Ghosts, goblins, and corpses roused by spirits
also roam about. In an empty house

at the crossroads
they hope to unnerve the devotee.

A half-moon on his forehead
a big trident in his hand
clumps of matted hairs falling to his feet
the police chief is arrogant
like Death.
First he resembles a snake
then a tiger
then a huge bear!

This may alarm the devotee:
Ghosts will kill me!
I can't sit a second more!
He's turning toward me
blood-red eyes!

But can a true practitioner
fall into danger? The police chief is pleased:
"Well done! Well done! Kālī
of the Grisly Face
has empowered your mantra.
You've conquered
now and forever!"

Poet Rāmprasād the slave
floats in a sea of bliss.
What can trouble a practitioner?
Are frightful scenes a threat?
He stays sitting on the hero's seat,
with Kālī's feet
for a shield.

Rāmprasād Sen

12

The moon flashes in Her blessed face.
God oh God—how lovely!
I saw Her and blanked out;
shame on me!
I failed to offer *javā* flowers at Her feet.

He who installs the Mother on earth
is a king of men, a great ruler.
Twice-born Rāmkṛṣṇa is a good protector of the land;
I have crossed over this world and the next.

Mahārāja Rāmkṛṣṇa Rāy

13

Who is this,
dressed like a crazy woman,
robed with the sky?
Whom does She belong to?
She has let down Her hair,
thrown off Her clothes,
strung human hands around Her waist,
and taken a sword in Her hand.
Her face sparkles
from the reflection of Her teeth,
and Her tongue lolls out.
The smile on that moon-face drips
heaps and heaps of nectar.

Mother,
are You going to rescue Kamalākānta
in *this* outfit?

Kamalākānta Bhaṭṭācārya

14

Oh hey, All-Destroyer,
which corpses did You raid for ash
  to come here smeared like this?
Don't You have a place to play
  that's not a crematorium?
Oh Wild-Haired One,
  You tousle Your hair and wander at will.
If I follow You
even a moment
  I get no peace.

Oh bone-burning bothersome girl!
Where did You get Your necklace of bones?
And why, when the cream of Your skin
bewitches the world,
do You arrive here
plastered with soot?
With tears from my eyes
I'll wash off Your smut;
come, Mā, to my lap.
Yet even when I hold You to my chest,
still I die of pain;
that's why I abuse You, Mā.

Najrul Islām

15

Kālī
is everything You do misleading?

Look, Your beloved has thrown Himself
under Your feet! Mother
I beg You with folded hands:
don't dance on top of Śiva!

I know how Tripura's Enemy feels.
Beautiful Tripurā, Kind Woman,
just this once, stop.
You're the murderer of Your own husband;
You're killing Your lord!
The King of Living Beings
is almost dead!

Once
hearing people criticize Śiva
You got angry
and left Your body
for love.

Mother! The man You're standing on
is the same Three-Eyed One!
Calm down
look at Him;
it's the Naked Lord!

This is what Kamalākānta wants to understand:
You know everything,
so why all these deceptions?
This time, I think,
You've gone too far,
You Whose Seat Is a Corpse.

Kamalākānta Bhaṭṭācārya

16

Kālī, what family are You from?
You're absorbed in Your own fun and games.

Who really understands Your incomparable beauty?
If I look at You
I can't tell day from night.
Though You're black
glossier than smeared mascara
You don't wear saris, gold, or jewels
Your hair's all tousled
and You're always at the cremation grounds
even so
my mind forgets all this
I don't know how.

Look! The Jewel of men
masses of matted hair and snakes on His head
is *He* devoted to Your feet?
Who are You to Him? Who is He to You?
Who would ever guess
that the Crest-Jewel of the gods
the Shelter of the shelterless
the Entertainer of the universe
would cling to Your feet
as the most cherished treasure?

Kamalākānta can't comprehend Your endless virtues.
The earth and sky are lit by Your beauty.

Kamalākānta Bhaṭṭācārya

17

It's not Śiva
at Mother's feet.
Only liars say that.

Mārkaṇḍeya wrote it clearly
in the *Caṇḍī*:
while killing demons,
saving the gods from their fix,
Mā stepped on a demon child
fallen to the ground.
At the touch of Her feet
the demon boy changed;
suddenly he was Śiva
on the battlefield.

As a good wife
would She ever
put Her feet
on Her husband's chest?
No, She wouldn't.
But a servant is different:
Rāmprasād pleads—

place those fear-dispelling feet
on my lotus heart.

Rāmprasād Sen

18

How can that black woman be so beautiful?

Fate has made Her the color of a new cloud.
She laughs horribly
lightning darting from Her teeth, yet
what a lot of nectar drips
from Her moon-face!

The sun shines in Her *sindūra* dot,
that lotus face

beguiling even the God of Love.
Sun, fire, and moon
sattva, *rajas*, and *tamas*
have risen
reddish
in Her three eyes.

Her navel is a lotus swaying
inside a lake, where water lilies
bloom into breasts. Her thick hair
streams down Her body, a garland of heads
hanging around Her neck. Even those earrings
children's corpses
look stunning against the Mother's ears.

Ornament after ornament
adorns Her beautiful feet,
Her toenails shaming the moon
by their mirrorlike gleam.

Seeing such a sweet form
Kamalākānta goes to Śyāmā's very spotless feet
for refuge.

Kamalākānta Bhaṭṭācārya

19

Kālī!
Today in the dark grove
creepers with their crimson shoots
are a fiery mass.
Anklets tinkle, bees hum,
cuckoos sweetly sing.

On Her head is a peacock's crown,
at Her ears, *vihaṅgī* bird ornaments.
Her navel is a white lotus
and She has restless *khañjana* bird eyes.
Bees sip nectar
from Her flowery face.

With *tamāla* trees for legs, ankleted
with snakes,

She stands on Śiva
    the silver mountain.

Kamalākānta,
look at this great wonder:
Śaṅkarī on the chest
            of Śaṅkara.

Kamalākānta Bhaṭṭācārya

20

Use your mental eye
and see
    Śyāmā's matchless form:

She's brilliant like lightning
cleaving black clouds,
and the sun and moon, clouds and stars,
hover at Her feet. In the three worlds
She's beautiful beyond compare, and so sweet,
with moons by the thousands in Her toenails, and serpents
twined for braids, ducking down
    always hiding
one taking space from another.

Stay like this, my Three-eyed Mother,
and dance!
                        Dance in bliss,
Ever-Blissful Best of Women
    on Nīlkaṇṭha's lotus heart.
Beat the sweet *mṛdaṅga* drums, make music on the vina.
And sing the name of Hari
in modes and measures.

Nīlkaṇṭha Mukhopādhyāy

The Cosmic Goddess of Transformation

In this section, the Goddess's principal epithet is Brahmamayī, She Who Is Filled with Brahman, or Whose Essence Is Brahman. As such, she has the ability both to encapsulate and embody all forms as well as to transcend them. Her forms, when she chooses to take them, encompass the range of opposites: male and female, black and white and all colors in between, material and spiritual, beautiful and terrible. In addition, they include any of the chief deities of the Hindu (and even Muslim and Christian) traditions, although—possibly for purposes of countering the rival Vaiṣṇava cult—her poets have a particular preference for her identification with Kṛṣṇa. As poem 30 indicates, she also incarnates herself in human women.

That Brahmamayī can transform herself into such an array of beings is cause for the poets' wonder; they claim that she does so out of compassion for her worshipers, each of whom thinks of her in a different way, and out of the sheer joy at doing what she pleases. In any case, her abilities are beyond the ken of any living person, and many of the poems end with examples of the impossible, as a way of conveying how difficult it is to grasp the infinitude of the Goddess's transformative powers. Even the traditional sources of knowledge—the six philosophies, and the Vedas, Nigamas, Āgamas, and Purāṇas—cannot penetrate her being.[24] Only Śiva can claim such understanding.

21

Who can understand Kālī?
You can't get Her vision
through the six philosophies.

She plays with Śiva
two swans
amorous amidst lush lotuses.
Ascetics ponder Her
from *mūlādhāra* to *sahasrāra*.

Like "Oṃ," the root of all,
Kālī is the self
of one who delights in the self.
Just for fun
She dwells in body after body,
encasing our universe
in Her belly. Can you imagine
measuring *that*?
The Destructive Lord has grasped Her core,
but who else can?

Prasād says, People laugh at me
trying to swim across the sea.
My heart knows but my mind does not—and so
                    though a dwarf
I try to catch the moon!

Rāmprasād Sen

22

Is my black Mother Śyāmā really black?
People say Kālī is black,
but my heart doesn't agree.
If She's black,
how can She light up the world?
Sometimes my Mother is white,
sometimes yellow, blue, and red.
I cannot fathom Her.
My whole life has passed
                    trying.
She is Matter,
then Spirit,
then complete Void.

It's easy to see
how Kamalākānta
    thinking these things
went crazy.

Kamalākānta Bhaṭṭācārya

23

Mā, You're inside me;
who says You keep Your distance, Śyāmā?
You're a stony girl, terrible illusion,
dressing in many guises.
For different methods of prayer You put on
the five chief forms.
But once someone realizes
the five are one,
there'll be no escape for You!
Understanding the truth,
he won't encumber You with false worship
and You'll have to stop
as if You'd sneezed
to take his burdens.

Once he knows the value of gold
will he welcome glass
by mistake?

Prasād says, My heart is shaped like a flawless lotus.
I place You there, my mental Goddess:
Now dance!

Rāmprasād Sen

24

Mother,
You're always finding ways to amuse Yourself.

Śyāmā, You stream of nectar,
through Your deluding power
You forge a horrible face
and adorn Yourself with a necklace of skulls.
The earth quakes under Your leaps and bounds.
You are frightful
with that sword in Your hand.

At other times
You take a flirtatious pose,
and then, Mother,
even the God of Love is undone!

Your form is inconceivable and undecaying.
Nārāyaṇī, Tripurā, Tārā—
You are beyond the three qualities
        yet composed of them.
You are terrifying,
You are black,
You are beautiful.

Thus assuming various forms,
You fulfill the wishes of Your worshipers.
Sometimes You even dance
        Brahman, Eternal One
in the lotus heart of Kamalākānta.

Kamalākānta Bhaṭṭācārya

25

Kālī, Mā,
You're dressed as Rāsavihārī,
Vrindavan dancer!
Your mantras are various
and so are Your activities; who can grasp them?
                The subject is extraordinarily difficult.

Half Your body's matchless Rādhā,
    a woman, and the other half's a man—
a yellow cloth tied at Your waist,
Your wild hair knotted back, and a flute
    in Your hand.

Once You infatuated Tripura's Enemy
        stealing sideways glances at Him, but this time
it's women You tempt
    with Your beautiful black figure
        and hinting eyes.

Your laugh used to be dreadful;
it threw into a panic
the three worlds.
Now You speak sweetly.
Girls in Vraj swoon.
As Śyāmā, You danced in a sea of blood; today Your favorite waters are the Yamuna.

Prasād laughs, flooded with delight:
after thinking hard, I finally get it—
Śiva, Kṛṣṇa, and the black-bodied Śyāmā
they're all one
but nobody else can see it.

Rāmprasād Sen

26

Śyāmā Mother's lap a-climbing
speak I always Śyām's name.
Mā's become my *mantraguru*;
my Ṭhākur, though, is Rādhā-Śyām.
I dive into my Śyāmā-Yamuna,
and play there in the water
with my Śyām.
But when He hurts me and neglects me,
it's Mā who'll fill
the dreams I am.
On my heart, my instrument,
Śyām and Śyāmā are two strings;
playing at once inside myself,
that splendid "Oṃ"
forever sings.
With illusion's threads
Great Illusion binds
that teenaged Śyām
and brings Him here;
so in Kailasa I call Her Mā
but see the place as Vraj's sphere.

Najrul Islām

27

Oh Kālī Full of Brahman!
I've searched them all
        Vedas, Āgamas, Purāṇas
and found You:
Mahākālī
  Kṛṣṇa
        Śiva
          Rāma—
they're all You
my Wild-Haired One.

As Śiva, You hold a horn,
Kṛṣṇa a flute,
Rāma a bow,
and Kālī a sword.
You're the Naked Goddess
with naked Śiva, and the passionate Lord
robed in yellow.
Sometimes You live on burning grounds,
sometimes at Ayodhya, and also at Gokul.
Your friends are witches and terrifying spirits.
Just as, for the sake of the young archer
  You took the form of Jānakī, greatest beauty,
So You do for any boy, Ma:
become a girl.

Prasād says,
Like the smile of a beast with bared teeth
ascertaining the nature of Brahman is impossible.
But the essence of my Goddess *is* Brahman,
and She lives in all forms.
The Ganges, Gaya, and Kashi
        even they are arrayed at Her feet.

Rāmprasād Sen

28

I understand now, Tārā, I understand:
You're a master at magic.
However a person conceives of You,
You willingly assume that form:
the Burmese call You Pharātarā,
the Europeans call You Lord.
To Moguls, Pathans, Saiyads, and Kazis You are Khodā.
Śakti for the Śāktas,
Śiva for the Śaivas,
Sūrya for the Sauryas,
and Rādhikā-jī for the Vairāgīs.
To Gāṇapatyas You are Gaṇeśa,
to Yakṣas, Lord of Wealth,
to artisans, Viśvakarmā,
and among boatmen, Saint Badar.

Śrī Rāmdulāl says, This isn't trickery;
quite the opposite. It is I
reflecting on the divisions of the one Brahman
who makes the mischief!

Rāmdulāl Nandī

29

Mā, You are Brahmāṇī in the world of Brahmā,
Sarvamaṅgalā in Vaikuntha, Gayeśvarī in Gaya, and
Amarāvatī in Indra's world.
In Dakṣa's home You are Satī,
at Śiva's place His wife Pārvatī.

I hear they call You Vimalā in Puri.
But Mother of the World, show mercy
to sad and dejected me
and tell me this:
if at the bridge You are Rāmeśvarī and Kṣemaṅkarī,
and as Rājeśvarī You hold a skull-topped staff in Your hand,
where do You manifest as all-pervading Viśveśvarī?

At Vrindavan You are Kātyāyanī,
in the Himalayas You lived in Girirāj's house, Mā,
            fascinating Him.
You even wore a monster's guise
in Kaṃsa's birthing room!

Whatever form You take, Mā Śaṅkarī,
    whether Caṇḍī in Lanka
            or Bhuvaneśvarī in the netherworld
I can't understand Your play.
Mā Caṇḍikā, how did You defeat Śumbha and Niśumbha
                    or kill the buffalo demon with Your ten arms?

For Śrīmanta's sake You took a freakish form
    Kamalekāminī
while sitting in a lotus clump
in the deep waters of the sea.
Śāradā says,
            From that very lotus perch, Mā,
            You were engaged in swallowing elephants!?

Śāradā Bhāṇḍārī

30

Wherever there's a woman in any Bengali home
    doing her work
    screening her smiles with her veil,
she is You, Mā;
she is You, Black Goddess.

Carefully rising with the light of dawn
    to attend with softened hands
            to household chores,
she is You, Mā;
she is You, Black Goddess.

The woman who gives alms, makes vows, does worship, reads scriptures
            all correctly and with a smile
who drapes her sari over the child on her lap
soothing its hunger with a lullaby,
she is You, Mā;
she is You, Black Goddess.

She can't be anyone else;
mother, father, sister, housewife
all are You.
Even at death
smiling
You make the journey with us.
My mind knows this, and my heart as well:
she is You, Mā;
she is You, Black Goddess.

Mā Bāsantī Cakrabarttī

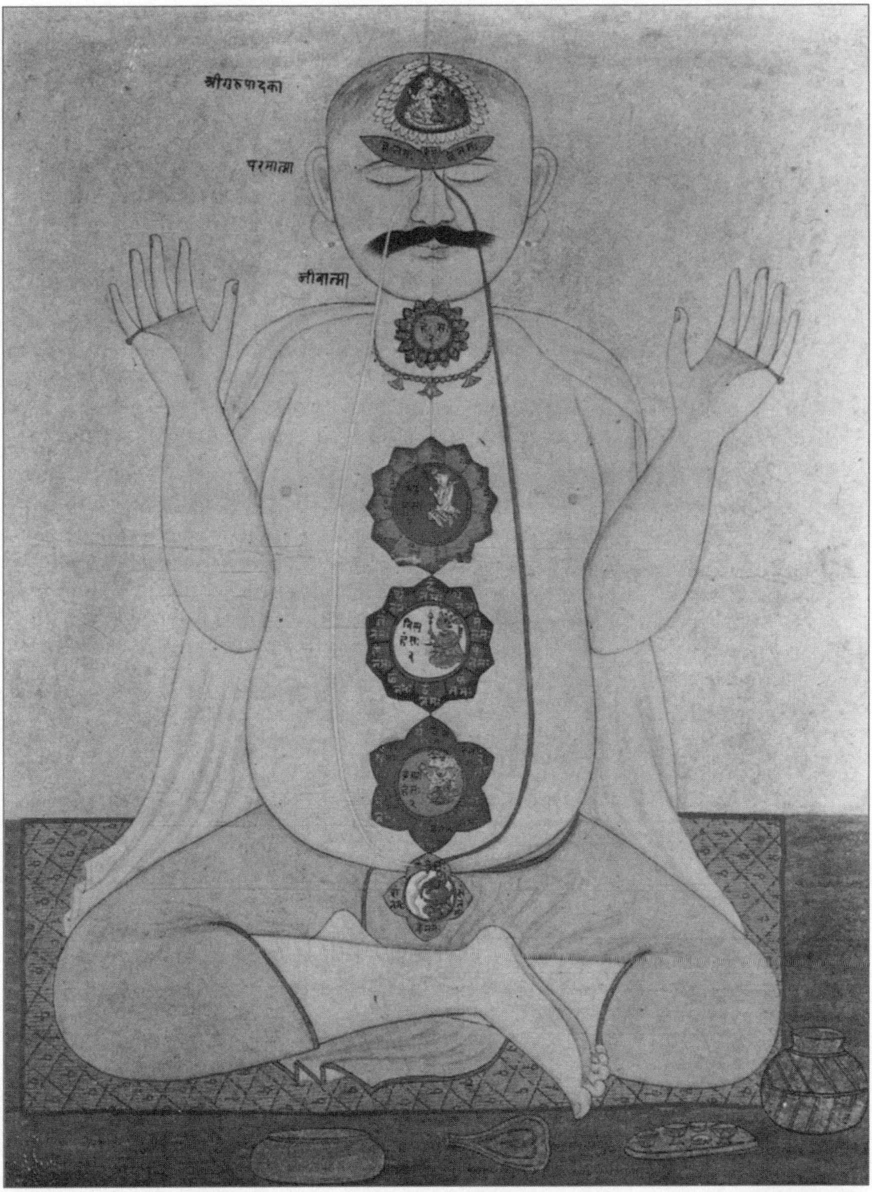

Figure 1. The subtle body according to *kuṇḍalinī* yoga. Kangra, Himachal Pradesh, ca. 1820. Gouache on paper. From the collection of Ajit Mookerjee. Reproduced by courtesy of the National Museum, New Delhi.

Figure 2. Kālī standing on Śiva. Kalighat, Calcutta, ca. 1855. Watercolor. From the collection of the British Library (Add. Or. 4527). Reproduced by permission.

	where situated in the body	number and color of petals; letters written on each	color and shape of interior zone	element and regnant sense organ	*bīja* mantra	resident male deity	resident female deity	resident animal
mūlādhāra	bottom of the spinal cord, under the genitals	four, red; *v, ś, ṣ, s*	yellow square	earth; smell	*laṃ*	Brahmā	Ḍākinī	elephant
svādhiṣ-ṭhāna	above the genitals	six, orange; *b, bh, m, y, r, l*	white crescent moon	water; taste	*vaṃ*	Viṣṇu	Rākinī	crocodile (*mākara*)
maṇipura	navel	ten, brown; *ḍ, ḍh, ṇ, t, th, d, dh, n, p, ph*	red down-pointing triangle	fire; sight	*raṃ*	Rudra	Lākinī	ram
anāhata	heart	twelve, vermilion; *k, kh, g, gh, ṅ, c, ch, j, jh, ñ, ṭ, ṭh*	smokey-grey six-pointed star	wind; touch	*yaṃ*	Īśa/Īśvara	Kākinī	antelope
viśuddha	throat	sixteen, light brown; *a, ā, i, ī, u, ū, ṛ, ṝ, ḷ, ḹ, e, ai, o, au, aṃ, aḥ*	white down-pointing triangle	space; hearing	*haṃ*	Sadāśiva	Śākinī	white elephant
ājñā	between the eyebrows	two, white; *h, kṣ*	white (no shape to internal zone)	mind	*oṃ*	Śambhu	Hākinī	(none)
sahasrāra	top of the head	one thousand (twenty layers of the entire fifty-letter alphabet), white	All prior dualistic elements, beings, and modes of worship are here subsumed and dissolved, when the *jīva* experiences the union of Puruṣa and Prakṛti, Śiva and Śakti					

Figure 3. A descriptive diagram of the seven *ċakras* in the subtle body.

Figure 4 (*above*). Durgā killing Mahiṣāsura. Kalighat, Calcutta, ca. 1855–1860. Watercolor. From the collection of the Victoria and Albert Museum (IM.2:79—1917). Reproduced by permission.

Figure 5 (*right*). Śiva, Pārvatī, and Gaṇeśa. Kalighat, Calcutta, ca. 1830. Watercolor. From the collection of the Victoria and Albert Museum (IS.207—1950). Reproduced by permission.

Figure 6. Annapūrṇā seated, giving rice to Śiva. Kalighat, Calcutta, ca. 1855–1860. Watercolor. From the collection of the Victoria and Albert Museum (IM.2:74—1917). Reproduced by permission.

Figure 7 (*above*). Pārvatī taking her son Gaṇeśa to her mother's house. Kalighat, Calcutta, ca. 1885. Watercolor. From the collection of the Victoria and Albert Museum (IS.577—1950). Reproduced by permission.

Figure 8 (*left*). Umā leaving the house of her mother. Kalighat, Calcutta, ca. 1885. Watercolor. From the collection of the Victoria and Albert Museum (IS.588—1950). Reproduced by permission.

The Magician's Daughter and Her Playful Deceptions

The Śākta Goddess is not only terrifying and all-pervading; she is also, as the creator of the universe, the cause of human bondage. The embodiment of illusion, who ensnares us in worldly attachments (*māyā*), she is adept at magic, sorcery, and secrecy, and her relation to the world is one of self-absorbed play (*līlā*). As such, she determines our actions. For some poets, this appears not to be a theological problem; Naracandra, in poem 31, admits her control with approbation. Most others, however, reprove their Goddess. If she has foreordained what we think, do, and say, then she cannot rightly blame us for our ineptitudes. Several of the poems that follow end on notes of sarcasm or critique.

And yet there is another side to this Goddess of illusion. If she enmeshes us, she can also free us; hence the refusal to abandon her or to cease hoping in her saving grace. Because she is so unpredictable, she may yet choose to be kind. As Kamalākānta says in poem 33, if it were not for Kālī's gentler side, he would never persevere in her worship.

Note the obvious dependence of later poets, in this case Kamalākānta, upon the linguistic and theological precedents set by Rāmprasād (poems 32 and 33).

31

Everything is Your wish, Tārā,
You Whose Wish Is Law.
You do Your own work,
but people say, "I am acting."
You make the elephant get stuck in mud,
the lame man leap across mountains.
To some You give the heights of Indra;
others You push down to hell.
I speak the words You make me speak.

You are mystic diagrams
You are mystic words;
You are the essence of the *Tantrasāra*.

Naracandra Rāy

32.

What's the fault of the poor mind?
Śyāmā, You're the magician's daughter;
it dances as You make it dance.
You are action, virtue, and vice;
I've figured out Your secret.
Mā, You are earth, You are water;
You make fruit
ripen on the tree.
You are power, You are devotion;
You are even liberation,
says Śiva.
You are suffering, You are happiness;
so it's written in the *Caṇḍī*.

Prasād says,
The thread of attachment
is spun by action's wheel.
Crazy Kālī and crazy Śiva
bind souls with it
and make them play.

Rāmprasād Sen

33

What's the fault of the poor mind?
Why blame it unnecessarily?
It dances as the magician's daughter
makes it dance.

You have heard
She is merciful to the afflicted.

People say it's in the Vedas.
But how can One who forgets Herself
ever notice the pains of others?

She's the daughter of a cheat,
so Śiva's a great match for Her;
He goes around naked, smeared with ashes,
lest people say anything good about Him.

Nevertheless
Kamalākānta has surrendered his life
to Her feet. Apart from them
there is nothing. Otherwise, why *ever*
would he regard Her feet
as the essence of all?

Kamalākānta Bhaṭṭācārya

34

Ever-blissful Kālī,
Bewitcher of the Destructive Lord,
Mother—
for Your own amusement
You dance,
clapping Your hands.

You with the moon on Your forehead,
really You are primordial, eternal, void.
When there was no world, Mother,
where did You get that garland of skulls?

You alone are the operator,
we Your instruments, moving as You direct.
Where You place us, we stand;
the words You give us, we speak.

Restless Kamalākānta says, rebukingly:
You grabbed Your sword, All-Destroyer,
and now You've cut down evil *and* good.

Kamalākānta Bhaṭṭācārya

35

Oh Mā Kālī, for a long time now
You've masqueraded in this world
as a clown.
But I am punished inside,
and there's nothing funny about Your jokes.
Oh Mā, sometimes You're the air we breathe,
sometimes the sky in the seventh underworld
furthest away, and
sometimes the water in the sea.
You assume so many forms!
I have traveled to countless lands
and worn countless costumes; even so,
Your marvels—ha!—never cease.

Premik says,
My mind is a cad; that's why it's sunk
in attachments. Why else
would these tricks of Yours
keep working?

Mahendranāth Bhaṭṭācārya

36

Look here—
it's all the woman's play,
secret,
Her intentions Her own.
In the controversies over *saguṇa* and *nirguṇa*,
She breaks one lump of clay with another.
In all matters this woman is equally willing to help
except when you really need Her.

Prasād says, Sit tight
and float a raft on the Ocean of Becoming.
When the high tide comes, move upstream, and
when the waters ebb, go down.

Rāmprasād Sen

37

Brother,
this world
is nothing but a bamboo box,
so I roll about in it
        my bazaar of bliss.

Earth, water, fire, wind, and sky:
these five make an ordered world.
First gross matter
then consciousness, together
produce myriad forms
        like suns, multiplied
        on water in earthen bowls.
But without the bowls
                there's just one sun.

I sat like an ascetic in the womb,
but now that I've fallen to the ground
I swallow dirt. A midwife
cut my umbilical cord; who am I
    to cut illusion's chains?
Women charm
speaking sweetly
but there's poison, not nectar, in that cup.
In the past I drank
to my heart's content; now I writhe
burning with venom.

Rāmprasād says with joy,
Primordial Woman of the Primordial Man:
do whatever You please, Mother,
You—the daughter of a stone.

Rāmprasād Sen

"What Kind of a Mother Are You?" Cries of Complaint

Poems in which devotees tease, criticize, or roundly abuse the Goddess for her behavior and appearance are among the most lively and interesting of the Śākta Padāvalī corpus. She is indicted on four major counts: she does not live up to the promises inherent in her various names—the Compassionate, the Thoughtful, the Giver of Food, and so on; she exhibits none of the virtues proper to a mother, who is not supposed to show favoritism in her treatment of her children; she appears to have inherited all of the hard-heartedness of her stony father, the Himalaya Mountain; and she does not dress or behave in a fashion befitting a demure wife and mother. What makes all of these deceptions worse, say the poets, is that Śiva and the various scriptures have claimed that she is otherwise, leading devotees into false worship. Many of the *bhaṇitās* conclude with bitterness and sarcasm; no one would worship this Goddess if there were an alternative.

Even the most pungent comments, however, belie a deeper commitment. In spite of her demeanor, the poets refuse to let go of their Goddess, crying that, if nothing else, their steadfast devotion to her kinder side will save them in the end. As such, it is they who are the moral victors in these particular songs.

It is a point of some contention in the Bengali secondary literature as to whether one should interpret these poems as indicating the material circumstances of their composers. How much experience did Rāmprasād have with the workings of a law court, or with land sale agreements in country estates? Was he really poor and hungry? Was Kamalākānta in constant pain? Although we will never know for sure, due to the paucity of surviving historical information, it seems safest to assume that these were poetic conceits, metaphors and images drawn from the world at large to illustrate spiritual doubts and yearnings.

38

I'll die of this mental anguish.
My story is unbelievable;

what will people say
when they hear it?
The son of the World-Mother
is dying of hunger pangs!
The one You keep in happiness,
is he Your favorite child?
Am I so guilty
that I can't even get a little salt
with my spinach?
You called and called me,
took me on Your lap,
and then dashed my heart
on the ground!

Mother,
You have acted like a true mother;
people will praise You.

Rāmprasād Sen

39

Let me tell You a thing or two, Tārā,
about suffering.

Who says You're Compassionate to the Wretched?
Mā, to some You give wealth and family;
they win battles with chariots and elephants.
Others have the fortune
to be day laborers
unable to get spinach
with their meal.

Some live in buildings—
I also wish for that.
Mā, are they so terribly respect-worthy
and I a mere nothing?

Some wear two shawls, and eat their rice with sweet yoghurt.
Others are destined
for sandy spinach and parched rice mixed with husks.
Some get carried on palanquins;
I bear burdens.

Mā, what have I done? Spoiled
Your ripe harvest
with my rake?

Prasād says,
Because I forget You
I burn in pain.
Mā, I wish I were the dust
under Your fear-dispelling feet.

Rāmprasād Sen

40

What shall I say to You, Śaṅkarī?
I am speechless at Your behavior.
You play the part of the World-Mother,
but Your son has no clothes. Worse,
You dance on that corpse Śiva
engrossed in Your own thoughts.
I have so many sad things to say:
my Mother is the Queen of the Universe,
but me She has made a coolie
bearing loads in the
meaningless marketplace of the world.
You may not be ashamed of this,
but *I* am dying of shame.

Premik says, This naked Mother of mine
ruins me through shame.
You have given me so much pain, Mā,
but still I forget it all,
still I call You: "Mā Mā!"
Where else shall I stand?
I'll stop all this sulking; just listen, Mā, Mountain's Daughter:
if I can die with "Kālī!" on my lips,
I'll split the *brahmarandhra*
and be free.

Mahendranāth Bhaṭṭācārya

41

Let's be girls, Mā,
and play with dolls;
come into my playroom.
I will take the Mother's role, so I can
teach You how.

If You make one dull or wretched,
hold him to Your bosom;
who else will ease his pain?
One who gets no jewels and gems, Mā,
at least should get his mother.

Some will be quite naughty,
others lie about inside their homes,
but all play games of hide-and-seek
(our world here has no death, Mā),
crying as they leave at night, returning with the morning.

This little boy,
You made him cry
You made him fear.
Now love away his fear,
cease to make him cry—

or casting You aside
he'll run away.

When this play is finished
lull him into sleep;
hold him in Your arms.

Najrul Islām

42

Kālī, You have removed all my difficulties.
Whatever the Lord has written in my destiny
You have the power to fulfill it
or change it.
If You are merciful to someone

he shines with a supernatural luster.
He wears a loin cloth below his waist,
ashes on his body
and matted hair on his head.
A cremation ground makes him happy;
he has no interest in a house of jewels.
That master is like You—
always grinding the *siddhi* plant.

Whether You keep me happy or sad,
will I gain
making caustic comments?
I chose to be branded;
can I wipe off the mark now?

You have proclaimed
throughout the world
that Kamalākānta is Kālī's son.
But what kind of behavior is this
between Mother and son?
Who can understand it?

Kamalākānta Bhaṭṭācārya

43

Victory to Yogendra's Wife, Great Illusion!
Your glory is limitless!

I've heard that
just once if someone shouts
"Durgā Durgā Durgā!"
You take him across the sea of becoming.
So here I am
at the shore of the world
shouting "Durgā Durgā Durgā!" in my distress.
But where is Durgā, Mā? Where is She?
If You aren't partial to Your child, Mā,
and don't show me mercy,
then Your heart's a stone, Umā.
Is this the way a Mother acts?

Because I was a bad son
You became a bad Mother—what a fate!
But I guess You're acting in character

being born into a family of stones.
Oh Compassionate One! Today will You show mercy?
When, and to whom,
have You ever been kind?

Oh Śyāmā, All-Destroyer,
I know what concentrating on Your feet does to a man:
Brahmā became a celibate with a staff,
Śrī Hari abandoned everything
to float on a sea of milk,
and Śiva vacated His golden Kashi,
taking up residence at a crematorium
in renouncer's clothes!

Only Your name is Compassion. You
are empty of it.
Mā, You were Dakṣa's daughter once.
You went to his sacrifice, but when You saw
Śiva's absence, You got so insulted, aggrieved,
that You broke up the proceedings.
You weren't very nice to Your royal father.
You killed Yourself
and also him
without a thought for his feelings.

At Dakṣa's house
an insult to that man
upset You enough to leave Your body.
Now You stand on His chest,
Umā,
Hard-hearted.

Whether You save me
or don't, I'll use Your virtues
myself to cross over, with the boat of Durgā's name.
I'll keep it in excellent repair.
At the end, when Death comes
before my breathing stops
I'll cry out
"Durgā! Durgā!"

But Mā, Your *sādhana*'s unappealing;
whoever does it becomes poor.

Even if you call on Tārā once
you sink. This is not
a Mother's behavior!

Mā, at the end, in his war with Raghunātha,
Rāvaṇa the King called out to Durgā.

But You didn't look at him
or think of his suffering;
You destroyed him, Bhagavatī;
You were mean to a devotee.
And to finish things up,
You burned his lineage
not one saved.

He thought he had no cause for fear;
he played the kettledrum: "Victory to Kālī!"—
that drum was so brilliant—
but You feigned Your feelings
and burned his golden Lanka to the ground.

Oh Compassionate One!
When, and to whom,
have You ever been kind?

Anthony Sāheb

44

From now on,
don't deprive me any more, Tārā.
Look, the danger of death is near.
What You've done to me was appropriate.
I endured, it endured.
But now I must think:
what is the recourse for a wretched man?
Death is not conquered,
But I am not afraid;
I only worry lest I forget Your name
at my going.

Even though Kamalākānta is in pain,
he will smile.
Otherwise people will say
You haven't given me any happiness,
Śyāmā.

Kamalākānta Bhaṭṭācārya

45

Tārā, You are Cintāmayī, Full of Thought,
but do You ever give me a thought?
In name You Worry for the World,
but Your behavior is something else!
At dawn You make me think of the day's troubles,
at mid-day I concentrate on my stomach,
at night, on my bed,
I worry about everything.
Speak to me, Mā; I'm always calling You:
at first I thought I had You—
the One Who Becomes What One Thinks
Who Surpasses All Thought
but then You lost all thought for Śambhucandra,
and gave him the slip.

Kumār Śambhucandra Rāy

46

Tārā, what more are You planning?

Oh Mā,
will You keep giving me
the same comforts
You've furnished in the past?
If Śiva tells the truth
why should I have to appease You?

Mā, oh Mā,
You deceive me, and then deceive me again;
my right eye throbs in vain.
If I had any other shelter
I'd never entreat You.

Mā, oh Mā,
You gave me hope, then abandoned me—
helping me up a tree
before snatching the ladder away.

Prasād says,
There's no doubt in my mind:
Dakṣiṇākālī is extremely severe.
Mā, oh Mā,
my life is over, done for;
I've paid You my fee.

Rāmprasād Sen

47

I know, I know, Mother:
You're a woman of stone.
You dwell inside me,
yet You hide from me.

Displaying Your illusory power,
You create many bodies,
with Your three qualities
limiting the limitless.

Kind to some,
harmful to others,
You cover Your own fault
by shifting the blame to others.

Mother, I don't hope for enlightenment,
nor do I wish to live in heaven.
I just want to visualize Your feet
standing in my heart.

Oh Goddess Filled with Brahman,
this is Kamalākānta's humble appeal:
why do You harass him unnecessarily?
What is Your intention?

Kamalākānta Bhaṭṭācārya

48

Can someone
called Daughter of a Stone
have compassion in Her heart?

If She weren't pitiless, could
She kick Her husband in the chest?

The world knows You
as the Compassionate, but
there isn't a trace of compassion
in You. You wear a necklace
of heads, cut
from other mothers' sons!

The more I cry "Mā Mā!"
the more
        though I know You hear me
You don't listen.
Prasād gets kicked
for no reason. Still
he calls out
                "Durgā!"

Rāmprasād Sen

49

Your behavior proves how stingy You are, Mā.

You always give to Your devotees—
        or so I've heard from the Āgamas.
You who gave rise to the world,
        tell me—what did You give to whom?
In the very act of giving
You bind people in the net of illusion
        and give them pain.
I've heard Your name
        Full of Food
but that Trident-Bearer is a beggar!
He was so hungry
He had to eat poison—
        naked, with nothing on!
If You're really Kubera's Mother,
as people say,
        why do You have a necklace of bones
        at Your throat?

Oh Goddess draped with the snakes of death,
the extent of Your riches is well known.

Premik says, Oh Mā Kālī,
it hurts me to say this:
I don't want money, Śyāma,
so since You can't give me any
it's all right. But You aren't even able
to grant me Your vision!

Mahendranāth Bhaṭṭācārya

50

Mā, I've drunk Your poisoned nectar
and now I'm set to die
staggering, horrified
by Your many forms, All-Destroyer.
I think on Kālī's name
alas! and sink
with all my hopes of happiness
deep into a black pond's black waters.
Presuming it nectar
I dove into poison most deadly
and burn in its blaze.

Mā, You used to live in Hara's house;
You were Umā, the Mountain's Daughter.
Now I see Your bloody sword,
Woman with the Wild Hair,
and turn black in fear.
I thought You removed fear,
so I made a home
on the burning grounds. But what is this You have done
to Dīnrām, Mā,
appearing as the All-Destroyer?

I took shelter with You;
I craved fearlessness.
But I'm dying of fear.

Dīnrām

51

I'm not a child any more, Śyāmā;
now I'm Kālī.

I'll grasp Your sword of knowledge, and show
You the fear of death!
That necklace of skulls I'll snatch from Your neck
to wear on my own.
With a blazing passion
igniting the cremation grounds
I'll dance and clap my hands.
Darkness I'll build out of pain;
then You'll see how deeply I suffer.
I'll decorate Your body with fire, Mā,
burning from my three afflictions.
If Śiva is so compassionate,
how come You're so unkind?
I'm going to pinch Your basket full of offerings
and give You an empty one instead.

Bhadreśvar Maṇḍal

52

Out of love for You
I have put aside my passions.
You're a brazen woman
making love in the dominant position.
You've got no shame, no clothes,
and Your hair flies all over the place.
It is You, All-Destroyer,
who sets fire to creation.
I smear my body
with the ash from those cinders
that disgrace.

In the eye of time
passion is a fleeting illusion.
It rises on Tuesday and sets on Saturday.
Dīnrām investigates these things and puts his passions aside.

Let me stand at Your feet, Mā,
the only place that truly exists.

Dīnrām

53

Mā, if You wore a Benarasi sari
and tied up Your hair,
You'd look so good—
                    and there'd be no harm in it, Mā,
                    no harm at all.

If instead of standing on Daddy
You sat next to Him,
exchanging Your fearful form
for a sweet smile,
if there were no blood smeared on Your body,
                    You'd look so good—
                    and there'd be no harm in it, Mā.

What if Forgetful Daddy didn't lie
like a corpse at Your feet
but spoke to You honeyed words?
Think how nice that would be!
The whole world I am sure
would be astonished: Śiva and Kālī
are playing new games
          such an improvement!
                    You'd look so good—
                    and there'd be no harm in it, Mā.

Mā Bāsantī Cakrabarttī

54

I have learned:
Kālī's court is extremely unfair.
Someone's always shouting
"Accuser! Complainant!"
but nobody ever shows up.

How do you explain a court
where the bench clerk
is the top man?
The financial steward is deranged;
can you trust what he says?
I have brought in one lakh lawyers;
Mother, what more can I do?
I call You "Tārā,"
but I see my Mother has no ears.
I rebuke You:
You've gone deaf and become black.

Rāmprasād says,
She has disgraced my life.

Rāmprasād Sen

55

This is a fine mess:
we made an honest agreement
I'd pay rent on this land
but You falsified the land sale deed
dividing up into six
what should have been land just for me.
Since being born here
I've had to live with their sarcasm.
You made me survey the land, Mā, so I
mapped it out from corner to corner
just in time to pay my rent.
But hey, Śambhu—
look what kind of child Kālī has!

Prasād says,
Oh Mā Tārā,
now the tables have turned:
I've paid up the right number,
but instead of rupees
I've used coins valued at a quarter!

Rāmprasād Sen

Petitioning the Compassionate

The first two poems of this section are quite similar to those classed as "complaint," except that they conclude not with defiance but with supplication. Others are more thoroughly petitionary, stressing the poets' worthlessness, lack of love, and entanglement with the five senses and six enemies, and begging the Goddess for material, spiritual, and even political benefits. Her chief epithets stress her giving role (many end in -dā, "the Giver of") and her ability to save her supplicants by carrying them over the wide and stormy sea of existence (Tārā and its derivatives). The boat for this vital but dangerous journey is the Goddess's feet, the focus of great adoration; sometimes Śiva is the poet's rival in their pursuit.

In general, these poems are simple and straightforward, with the Goddess's devotees begging for mercy, grace, and managed devotion—that is, that she take the responsibility for overseeing and directing what issues from their hearts.

56.

Tell me, Śyāmā:
how could it hurt You to look at me
just once?
You're a Mother;
if You see so much pain
but aren't compassionate
what kind of justice is that?
I have heard from the scriptures
that You rescue the fallen.
Well? *I* am such a person—
wicked and fallen!

You are famed as a deliverer of the wretched.
If it pleases You,
take Kamalākānta across.

Kamalākānta Bhaṭṭācārya

57.

Tārā, this is why I call upon You
lest Śiva's words prove to be false
and You trick me at the end.
Śiva says in the Tantras
that if one takes Tārā's name one will be liberated.
So why am I still fallen in this world?

Tāriṇī Brāhmaṇī says,
Listen, Bhavānī:
at the end
let me see those red feet.

Tāriṇī Debī

58.

Now I'll see whether Śiva
can keep His ancestral treasure!
Whatever I'm fated to have
I'll fight Him for
and snatch it away.
I'll hit Him in the chest with my arrows
devotion and spiritual practice
fired from my victorious bow of knowledge.
As soon as I've shot Him
I'll run and grab those feet, my head
bowed to touch them. That treasure
will free me: no more fear of death.
Then I'll exit
beating my drum and yelling
"Victory to Durgā!"

I'm my father's son, and I'll fight Him, Mā;
all the gods can watch.

It's clear, I hear, in the *Rāmāyaṇa*
how Lava and Kuśa fought their father
in Vālmīki's forest, and won.
Now I've thought about this, Mā, and

made up my mind:
I'm going to draw my battle bow,
    fit the arrow of devotion into it,
        and beat that Three-Eyed Lord.

My spiritual practice may not be very powerful,
Mā Full of Brahman, but
        let Śiva be warned:
if I can overthrow Him
with my mantra
I will. In this battle
whatever happens happens.

Oh Mā Durgā, Destroyer of Obstacles, Wife of Hara!

We're in an evil age, Mā, and
I'm afraid of death.
But I've stepped onto the path;
I want liberation.
I'll perform the prescribed austerities
            loving You.

You are Primal Power, Emancipation-Giver,
Maker and Mother of the World,
Daughter of the Mountain, Highest Self, Eternal Brahman—
Mā! It's as clear as can be
that liberation lies at Your feet.
        Well aware of this fact,
        Śiva holds them to His heart.

"Give it to me!" says Bholā,
making a fuss to get the treasure
        that belongs to *me*!
Why does He act like this, Mā Full of Brahman,
            pouring out His body at Your feet?

I am not that kind of child, Mā,
but how much longer will Bholā's words
deceive me? Father sees me
dressed for battle. "What a disgrace!" He says.
But why? Why worry about
dying in battle? Even if I lose my life
        I won't let go
        this treasure.

I know You're a Woman of War,
and I'm Your son.

When You are present,
what's to fear? Best of all
is my teacher's gift:
    the arrow of devotion.

It's clearly said in the Purāṇas, Mother:
if you worship Śiva
    heaping Him with *bilva* leaves
He'll raise you to Himself
        out of kindness.
Aśvatthāmā, who won in battle,
testifies to this, Śyāmā.
And that's why it's said
Śiva's forgiveness proves His greatness.

If Hari says I must die,
there's no harm in that, Mā Full of Brahman;
            just please
                give Raghunāth Your feet
when he dies.

Raghunāth Dās

59.

Give me food,
        Mā Full of Food,
give me food,
        Food-Giver.
Oh Śāradā of my heart-lotus,
give me knowledge,
        Knowledge-Giver.

Blessed is Kashi, and Śiva too:
theirs the fallen river Ganges,
theirs the Goddess Filled with Food.

With folded hands I pray to You:
be good to me;
the pains of hunger hurt me, Mā.
Give me medicine to heal me: give me nectar.
And at the end
give me freedom at Your feet,
        Freedom-Giver.

Mahārāja Rāmkṛṣṇa Rāy

60.

Supreme Savior of Sinners,
awarding the fruit of highest bliss,
grant the shade of Your feet
to this very wretched one,
    Wife of Śaṅkara.

In Your great goodness
be merciful to me,
    Deliverer,
    Mā.

I've committed sins,
I've got no merit,
and as for prayer
I'm empty.
Take Your form Tārā
and rescue me,
    Mother of the Universe.

Your feet are my boat;
They carry me over the sea of becoming.
Be gracious to Prasād,
    Bhava's housewife.

Rāmprasād Sen

61.

The world's a shoreless ocean;
there's no crossing it.
But I bank on Your feet and the treasure of Your company—
rescue me, Tāriṇī,
in my distress.

I see the waves
    the bottomless waters
and shiver in terror:
I might drown and die!
Be merciful,

save Your servant,
harbor me now
        in Your boat
                Your feet.

The tempest storms without lull,
so too my shaking body.
I'm repeating Your name
        Tārā! the essence of the world.
Fulfill my desire.

Prasād says:
Time has passed
I haven't worshiped Kālī
and life is gone, unfruitful.
So free me from these worldly bonds.

Mother Tāriṇī,
without You
to whom shall I give my burden?

Rāmprasād Sen

62.

Tārā, Mother,
lift me out by the hair
and I'll be saved from this disaster.

This shore, that shore,
they're separated by the sea.
Swimming from one to the other
    is inconceivable.
I float along with my worthless companions.
If they want to catch hold of anything,
they grab *me*!
They sink, I sink; our lives are gone.
All my hopes
        the props I depended on
are unfulfilled. You enchanted me once;
tell me—
if I sink now,

what will You do next
and when?

Who else but the Mother
will bear the burden of Kamalākānta?
Mā! Give me shelter at Your feet;
take me home.

Kamalākānta Bhaṭṭācārya

63.

It's no one else's fault, Śyāmā Mā;
I'm drowning in waters
I made myself.
The six enemies took the shape of trowels
and helped me
such a fine piece of land!
to dig a well.
Oh You, Delighting the Heart of Time,
that well filled up with the waters of time.
Now what will happen to me,
Tāriṇī, Embodiment of the Three Primordial Properties?
I've lost all virtue through my own choices.
How can I stop up the waters?

Dāśarathi ponders this, eyes filling
with unstoppable tears. The waters
flooded my house;
soon they rose up to my chest.
From life to life there's no escape.
But if You give me the lifeboat of Your feet,
Beneficent One,
I'll try to persevere.

Dāśarathi Rāy

64.

I've given up wanting
good relations with the world, Mā;
I just want that with You.

No more wandering
from fair to fair, paying out gold
    to buy virtue.
Fireworks at a fair
bursting in flame—
starry sparks and colored torches—
finish in a flash,
and I go home
    completely lacking revenue.
Bugs make homes in people's houses;
    I'm dying in pain from their poisoned chew.
My bed of love,
my quilt of feeling,
    they're broken down and torn askew.

There's no going back; and so I pray,
    Oh You Who Gives the Lost the Way,
if I fall at Your feet
let there be
        a special place for Dīnrām too.

Dīnrām

65.

Mother, make *me* Your treasurer;
I'm not the type to hurt my benefactor, Śaṅkarī.
I can't stand how everyone
loots the strong room
for Your jeweled feet.
That forgetful Tripurāri is supposed to be on guard,
but Śiva is appeased easily, and it's His nature
to give things away. In spite of this,
You keep Him in charge?
He's only responsible for half His body,
but His salary is nice enough.
I, however, am just a servant
and get no salary. The only claim
I have is the dust at Your feet.
If You take after Your father, then I'm lost,
but if You take after my father,
there's a chance I may get You, Mother.

Prasād says, I'll die for those feet.
If I get the job with them,
all dangers will cease.

Rāmprasād Sen

66.

How will You rescue me, Tārā?
There's only one of You,
but there are so many plaintiffs
I can't even count them!
You thought that because of my devotion
You could save me
by hook or by crook,
but the devotion of a nondevotee
is like a conch-shell marriage bracelet
on the arm of a slut. It's true
there is nothing more important
than the name of Brahman
but even that is a great burden for me.
My mind and my tongue think alike
only at mealtimes.

Kamalākānta's Kālī!
I'll tell You how to save me:
sit in my heart.
The only worthwhile solution
is for You to keep watch.

Kamalākānta Bhaṭṭācārya

67.

Because You love cremation grounds
I have made my heart one
so that You
Black Goddess of the Burning Grounds
can always dance there.
No desires are left, Mā, on the pyre

for the fire burns in my heart,
and I have covered everything with its ash
to prepare for Your coming.
As for the Conqueror of Death, the Destructive Lord,
He can lie at Your feet. But You, come, Mā,
dance to the beat; I'll watch You
with my eyes closed.

Rāmlāl Dāsdatta

68.

Wake up, Śyāmā, wake up, Śyāmā!
Appear once more as demon-chopping Caṇḍī!
If You don't wake up, Mā,
neither will Your children.

Oh Giver of Food! Your sons and daughters starve,
running here and there
more dead than alive. This sight
doesn't pain Your heart?

The cremation grounds You so love
today are the land of India.
Come, dance on this cremation ground;
breathe life into these skeletons.

For I desire, Mā, a free wind;
energy I desire; I desire long life.
Shake off Your sleep of delusion, Mā,
and wake up this Śiva—
You're surrounded by corpses!

Najrul Islām

"Oh My Mind!": Instructing the Self

When the Śākta poets are not petitioning or accosting the Goddess, they are doing the same to themselves. Their minds and their tongues—symbols of the self—are invited, advised, scolded, interrogated, urged, and warned to lead a more spiritual, Kālī-centered life. In particular, the poets exhort themselves to seek the Mother's feet, stealing them from Śiva and/or gaining them through devotion; to repeat her name, powerful over the fires of passion and sin, a present help in time of death; to see her presence in all things, events, and people; to note the marvels and miracles she has performed in people's lives; to revere her in her images and saints; and even to call upon her aid in political crises. Poems 88 and 89 are representative of the last two types of exhortation. In the former, Kālī is identified with the married saints, Rāmkṛṣṇa (1836–1886) and Śāradā Debī (1853–1920), residents of the Daksinesvar Temple in north Calcutta, whose love for Kālī has done an enormous amount to popularize the ritual worship and devotional cult of the Goddess since the end of the nineteenth century. Poem 89 was written during the 1905 partition of Bengal, and demonstrates the use of religious imagery for political purposes.

These poems are rich in metaphors for the material life in which the mind is enmeshed. The world is an estate; a farmer's field; a marketplace of taxes and capital losses; a stage; a springtime carnival; a game of dice; and a dangerous and billowy sea, where the boat is either the capsized, sinking poet or the Goddess, ready to save. Although the majority of poems depict the mind as dull, yearning after false hopes, crazy, and besotted with desire for sex, a few express the mental peace that comes through spiritual fulfilment.

In general, the poems in this section reflect three theological convictions: although the Goddess's grace is sufficient for liberation, until it is received mental effort is necessary; devotion is not a lower stage on the religious path but can lead to such liberation; and, as poem 83 claims, worldly experiences, though ultimately inessential, are useful aids in the pursuit of realization.

69.

Mind, let's go to an estate that's decent—
where people don't gossip about each other,
and where the *dewān* is a humble man
with ashes on his head
who doesn't feign devotion.
Even if you arrive there destitute
you'll be welcomed warmly;
they have no lack of money.

Dulāl says, But if you get into trouble there
the solution isn't money:
just tell Her attendants,
and the Compassionate One will show mercy.

Rāmdulāl Nandī

70.

Oh Mind, you don't know how to farm;
your human field has fallen fallow.
Cultivate it, and the crops you'll grow
will gleam like gold. Fence it round with Kālī's name
so your harvest won't be harmed.
The Wild-Haired One is strong;
Death won't come near that fence.
Don't you know? Your crops will never fail—
not in a day, a year, or a century.
So apply yourself, Mind;
work to reap your harvest.
The teacher sowed the mantra;
now water his seed with devotion's showers.
And oh, if you can't do it alone, Mind,
take Rāmprasād along.

Rāmprasād Sen

71.

It's silly to hope for Father's wealth.
Everything He owned
He deeded to someone else.
He gave all His money to Kubera
and sits around, completely mad.
I used to hope for Mother's feet,
but Father took them too.
And, lest anyone steal them,
He has placed them on His chest.
"When the father dies
the son inherits his wealth":
so say the scriptures.
But my Father has beaten death;
He isn't the dying type.

Rāmprasād Sen

72.

Talk to me, *javās*, talk to me—
what austerities did you do to get Śyāmā Mā's feet?
Torn from your stems on illusion's plants,
falling scattered to the ground at Her feet,
you got liberation
bursting open
beside yourselves with joy.
If only I could learn from your example
my life might bear fruit.
Thousands of sweet-smelling flowers bloom in the woods,
and they're all such beauties! So how come
you got Mā's feet?
You're just ignorant *javās*!

Crimson like you at the Mother's feet,
when will they be flowers
offered to Her, blessed by Her?
When will they turn red

at the touch of Her feet?
When will they, just like you, blush scarlet—
these dull petals of my mind?

Najrul Islām

73.

At last I have a way to understand
Kālī's blackness:
the black resin
that stains me in Her world.

Her movements are frenzied;
how can I tame Her?
I'll dance Her on my lotus heart
to mental music.
Mind, I can teach you
to get Kālī's feet.

As for those six saucy rogues
I'll chop them up. I'll spend my time
thinking Kālī,
being Kālī,
speaking Kālī.
At any time
good or bad
I'm set to smear soot
on Death's face.

Prasād says, Mā,
how much more can I say?
I'll take Your blows
and I won't fight back.
But nor will I stop
calling "Kālī!"

Rāmprasād Sen

74.

Oh my Mind, worship Kālī
any way you want—
    just repeat the mantra
        your teacher gave you
day and night.

Think that you're prostrating
as you lie on your bed, and
meditate on the Mother
while you sleep.
Go about town, and imagine
you're circumambulating Śyāmā Mā.
Each sound that enters your ears
is one of Kālī's mantras,
each letter of the fifty
around Her neck
bears Her name.

Rāmprasād says, astonished,
The Goddess Full of Brahman is in every creature.
When you eat,
think that you're making an offering
        to Śyāmā Mā.

Rāmprasād Sen

75.

Why should I sit alone, eyes closed,
    saying "Kālī Kālī"?
The One Garlanded with Heads stands in front of me
    in my range of vision.

Those heads around Her neck swing as She moves;
She's got children's corpses at Her ears
    javā flowers at Her feet.
Mā Mā—how happy I feel!
        Some say Mā sits on a corpse,
        but to me She appears in many different forms.

I've installed Her in the hearts of thousands;
I see Her with my eyes open.

For so long you were confused, Reṇu;
what were you thinking?
The Mother Who Takes away Fear
is here in front of me;
that's why to me
She isn't shocking.

Rāmreṇu Mukhopādhyāy

76.

The withered tree doesn't blossom.
I'm afraid, Mother:
it may crack apart!
Up in the tree,
I feel it sway back and forth
in the strong wind.
My heart trembles.

I had great hopes:
"I'll get fruit from this tree."
But it doesn't bloom
and its branches are dry.
All because of the six hostile fires!

As far as Kamalākānta is concerned,
there's only one recourse:
the name of Tārā destroys
birth, decay, and death.
Stamp out the flames with it,
and the tree will revive.

Kamalākānta Bhaṭṭācārya

77.

I started a fire with Kālī's name
in the forest Sin.
It raged, fanned by the wind

from my tongue.
The large trees, Lust and the like,
caught fire from each other
and burned to the ground.
The deer, all my evil thoughts—
how could they flee?
The birds, however,
who weren't much of a problem,
found an areal route of escape
in worship.

Kālī's name is so marvelous
that if you repeat it, practice it,
before long
all will be ash.

Āśutoṣ Deb

78.

Mā, the mail train is leaving now;
    it's time for it to go.
But I have no "ticket"
    and no credit,
        says the "Rail Bābu."
Without money I can't even
exit through the gate. So I guess
they'll tie up my hands,
and I'll sit on the "platform,"
    branded by the "Guard Bābu's" blows.

But when I listen inside
it seems someone is speaking in my ear:
"Why bother with a 'ticket'? Show your 'pass';
        rely on the strength of the name."
That's why at the end time
when destiny knocks
I'll speak that name
    and get a "first class" seat;
the "Checker Bābu" will go away
confounded.

Kalyāṇkumār Mukhopādhyāy

79.

Love Her, Mind;
She can ferry you across
the sea of birth and death.

Taxes must be paid in this worthless marketplace,
but it's stupid to trust in wealth and family.
Have you forgotten your past?
Where were you? Where have you come to?
Where are you going?

You wear nothing
but a costume in this world.
The Enchantress makes
illusion dance, so you dance.
And you sit on Her lap
in Her prison.

Egotism, hatred, love, attachment to pleasing things—
why did you share
your kingdom with these?
Tell me that!

What you've done can't be helped;
the day is almost over.
On a jeweled island
Śivā sits in Śiva's house.
Contemplate Her always.
Prasād says,
Durgā's ambrosial name liberates.
Repeat it without ceasing;
drench your tongue in nectar.

Rāmprasād Sen

80.

Crazy Mind,
you haven't been able to recognize
what a treasure Kālī is.
Just eating, sleeping, and having fun,

you waste your time, you crazy one.
You came into the marketplace of this world
hoping to trade.
What will happen now?
You seem to have lost your capital.
Through past merits you got a human body,
but what have you done about all those things
you had hoped to accomplish?

Kamalākānta's Mind!
Why have you come to this?
You're drowning in your own evil deeds,
and you're pulling me down as well.

Kamalākānta Bhaṭṭācārya

81.

Mind, I'm talking to you—
whose books are you keeping?
Did you become an accountant
to keep someone else's records?
If you did your own accounts
why didn't you keep an eye
on your profits, costs, overspending, and losses?
Day by day your expenses increase and your savings decrease.
Time is running out: settle your accounts—
the annual report is due.

Kumār says: Be precise with your figures
or you'll get a bad name. If you lose your profits
as well as your original investment
you'll become a debtor to Death.

Rāmkumār Nandī Majumdār

82.

Mind, why this separation from the Mother's feet?
Think on Her power

and you'll get liberation;
bind Her with the rope of devotion.

Though you had eyes
you didn't see. What bad luck
you have, my Mind!
The Mother tricked Her devotee!
Disguised as your daughter,
She helped you mend your fence.

At death you'll see
how much your mother really loves you.
She'll cry for an hour or two, then
purify the house with cow dung.
Brothers, friends, wife, children—
they're the core problem.
They'll donate a clay pitcher
and eight whole coins
for your corpse—after removing
from your body
whatever ornaments you were wearing
and covering you with an old cloth
torn in the middle and the corners.

He who meditates with undivided attention
on Kālikā Tārā
will get Her.
Come out and see the Goddess
Rāmprasād's daughter
mending his fence.

Rāmprasād Sen

83.

Oh my Mind! You're just spinning
around a Caḍak pole
in this grim world.

The great Lord of Yogis laughs at the joke,
but you don't recognize Him.
There are two self-born lingas
on every woman's chest, which you worship
with your five *bel*-leaf fingers!

At home you can listen to your wife; outside
at Śiva's Gājan festival, the big drums boom boom
and crowds of girls
dance the *khemṭā*.
You mounted the high pole of desire only to
fall on a spiked platform
    breaking your ribs.
Oh my Mind! You can ignore this pain, can you!?
        How lucky you are!
The Caḍak tree is tall with expectations; you feel it
to be the best of the best.
Oh my Mind, what you call love
is a fishhook threaded on a string of illusion.

Prasād will say it again:
The essential can grow from the inessential.
When you kick the bucket,
keep calling
        "Black Mā!"
and you'll get what you desire.

Rāmprasād Sen

84.

I came to this world
to play dice:
I had great expectations.
But my hopes were false
my condition deplorable:
the first throw was an unlucky five.
But then I started to do well:
thirteen, eighteen, sixteen.
In the end I got a twelve—one, five, and six—
but got stuck in the five and six!
Even worse, I threw a six and two and a six and four;
no one is under my control.
My playing was no success,
and now it's over;
my body's reached its limit.
There's no going further down that road.

Rāmprasād's intelligence is his weak point;
because he got stuck in the game,
he's going to have to start all over.

Rāmprasād Sen

85.

My Mind, my helmsman,
don't let the boat sink!
Don't let the rudder go!
Take courage; you can row across.
Mind, my oarsmen eyes
are outcastes—
insufferable! whatever they look at
distracts them.
    Śyāmā, the magician's daughter,
        has laid a good trap.
Mind, hoist the sail of devotion
in the wind of faith!

Rāmprasād says,
Sing a song about Kālī,
and press on.

Rāmprasād Sen

86.

Who can describe the waves of Mother Śyāmā's world?
I think I will swim upstream,
but who is pulling me back?
"I want to watch something funny," says my Mother,
and throws me in.
First I sink, then I float,
laughing inside.
The boat isn't far away;
it's near—
I can easily catch hold of it.

But this is my great dilemma:
shall I reach for it or not?
I am divided.

Kamalākānta's Mind!
Your desires are useless.
Take the boat;
if it is Tārā,
She may ferry you across
out of kindness.

Kamalākānta Bhaṭṭācārya

87.

Look at all these waves
whipped up in the ocean of my mind!
I see them and my mouth goes dry;
there's no escape.
Mind, the helmsman is an amateur
and the six enemies have taken the oars.
No one listens to what I say.
The situation is grave.
I see that they are working to sink us in mid-river.
The boat is constructed from five pieces of wood,
but there are holes in nine places.
It hasn't been repaired since it was built—
nor have the nine been stopped up.
Worse, the boat is heavy, filled with loads of sins.
I fear a crashing wave
will crack it apart.

Premik says, In this situation
keep the raft of Hari's name close by.
What's there to fear in a storm? It's just a temporary display.
When the boat sinks,
get onto the raft,
and by Hari's grace
you'll reach the other side.

Mahendranāth Bhaṭṭācārya

88.

Three Kālīs appeared in Daksinesvar
Go see Them with a full heart.
Go see Them with a full heart.
Three Kālīs appeared in Daksinesvar.

One Kālī, Bhavatāriṇī,
lives in the temple
built by Rāṇī Rāsmaṇī
    one of Rādhā's eight companions
        who came to earth for fun.
Go see Her with a full heart.
Go see Her with a full heart.
Three Kālīs appeared in Daksinesvar.

Another Kālī is Rāmkṛṣṇa; Rāmkṛṣṇa is His name.
He Himself
        though Kālī
never stopped calling "Kālī! Kālī!"
    grabbing Death by the hair
        in Syampukur.
Go see Him with a full heart.
Go see Him with a full heart.
Three Kālīs appeared in Daksinesvar.

Another Kālī is Mā Śāradā; Mā Śāradā is Her name.
As Kālī She served Kālī ceaselessly
    risking, in Telobhelo field,
        the dacoits' call.
Go see Her with a full heart.
Go see Her with a full heart.
Three Kālīs appeared in Daksinesvar.

Śyāmāpad Basu Rāy

89.

Come, brothers, everyone together:
with wreaths around our necks
let us worship Mother India

offering fruits
of our deeds for the country's improvement.
Risk even your life
for our home-grown goods.
Brothers, sons of the Mother all—
the white merchants shall weep
through our Movement.

Everything that once was India's own
is theirs; the plunder's complete;
eating, lying down, getting dressed—
in all
we humbly fall at their feet.

Develop distaste for those "pantaloons" and "coats";
instead wear the *dhuti*s made here.
As for "cigarettes," "enamel basins" for washing,
abandon them; don't hold them dear.

Now that they've split up Bengal,
the gloom of our error is past.
Curzon's conspiracy has made us aware;
reject foreign products; hold fast!
Let us all dress in Indian clothes,
singing "Victory to the Mother"
at last.

Mahendranāth Bhaṭṭācārya

90.

Black clouds have risen in my sky
and my mind my peacock
dances, prancing in joy.
Thundering "Mā! Mā! Mā!"
clouds clash
bedecking mountains
with lightning flashes—
smiles of bliss.

There's no stopping me, no rest for me:
water rains from my eyes
soothing my heart's thirsty bird.

After this life, there's the next
and so many still to come.

Not for me, says Rāmprasād:
no more births, no more wombs.

Rāmprasād Sen

Prioritizing Paths: Tantra, Devotion, and Ritual

Which is the best means to Kālī: Tantric yoga and meditation, devotion (bhakti), or ritual worship (*pūjā*) and pilgrimage visitation? As the poems in this section reveal, the Śākta poets do not sing in unison on this question; some claim that *kuṇḍalinī* yoga is the best spiritual practice, whereas others denigrate Tantra and meditation in favor of a simple, sincere, heartfelt love. What is common to both perspectives, however, is the disapproval of ritual worship, whether at the home temple or at some celebrated site; merely offering the Goddess flowers and goats will neither satisfy her nor gain the aspirant religious merit.

However, as a general rule, one will find more proponents of Tantric practice among the early poets than one will among their literary heirs. It is clear historically that Kālī and her fierce cognates arose from the Tantric world of ritual and philosophical speculation, and the Śākta poets of late-eighteenth- to early-nineteenth-century Bengal, such as Rāmprasād, Kamalākānta, and their zamindar patrons, were very aware of this. See poems 21 and 31, for example, where the practice of *kuṇḍalinī* yoga, as taught in Kṛṣṇānanda Āgambāgīś's *Tantrasāra*, is lauded as a mean of spiritual realization. The landed gentry of this period were keen to translate and patronize Tantric texts—quite a different situation from the mainly bhakti-oriented poets of the later nineteenth and twentieth centuries, for whom Tantra, like Vedic and philosophical knowledge, is rendered useless by devotion. Indeed, although there are exceptions (see the section after this), the farther away from the last quarter of the nineteenth century one gets, the less interest there appears to be in the intricacies of *kuṇḍalinī* yoga; what replaces it is praise for bhakti, championed as an easier, more accessible approach to the Goddess.

The poems in this section are arranged to reflect this gradual historical development. The first four (poems 91–94), three by Rāmprasād and one by Kamalākānta, compare rituals, pilgrimages, worship, and even devotion unfavorably with the knowledge gained through Tantric meditation. Even when Kālī's name is glorified, as in poem 93, it is within the context of *kuṇḍalinī* yoga, where one installs the Goddess in the heart lotus for reverential contemplation.

In poem 95, however, it is devotion that is juxtaposed with rituals and pilgrimage, not Tantra. In fact, things Tantric are put alongside rituals in the "inferior" category, as being useless or difficult, or leading to arrogance. Poems 96–98 explicitly deny that the Goddess can be found in Tantric texts or rites. Finally, leaving aside completely the critique of esoteric Tantra, the last five poems are straightforward in their exaltation of love over external, empty ceremony.

Note that although it is fairly uncommon for late-nineteenth- to twentieth-century poets to endorse Tantra over devotion, the reverse is not true for the earlier poets; Rāmprasād and Kamalākānta are represented on both sides of the Tantra/devotion divide, sometimes praising one, sometimes praising the other. One can account for this seeming contradiction in three ways: the poets may have changed their minds from time to time; not all of the poems attributed to them may have come from the same composer; and the lines between Tantra, devotion, and meditation may have been more blurred and indistinct than one might expect.

91

Tell me:
do you still want to trade, oh Mind?
Be content; do your austerities.
Then She'll owe you
        that Goddess Filled with Brahman
and you can collect your reward.

There's always air around a fan,
but only when you move it
do you feel the wind.
Oh Mind, that Goddess Filled with Brahman sleeps in your body;
stir Her up; wake Her.

If water gets in your ear, someone who knows the trick can drain it:
Oh Mind, he adds more water, and then it all comes out—
        or so the worldly say.

You house a great jewel,
but labor foolishly
in search of glass.
Oh Mind, the Lord gave you knowledge; hold onto it!
Open Time's door.
Then will be born
a strange being:
a grandson who kills old grandpa's wife.
Oh Mind, birth and death rituals, prayer, worship—
they're all just trouble.

Prasād says,
Not recognizing yourself, oh Mind,

is like dabbing vermillion
on a widow's forehead!
My God! What impeccable judgment!

Rāmprasād Sen

92

This time I've realized the essence:
I learned meditation from an adept.
I found someone from a country
where there's no night, and now
what good is morning?
what good is evening?
Twilight is barren for me.

I've shaken off sleep; will I go back to it?
Age after age I'm awake.
Now I've returned sleep to its maker
and lulled sleep to sleep.

With a mixture of borax and sulfur
I rub gold to make it shine.
In the same way I hope one day
to polish my temple of jewels.

Prasād says, I've held devotion and liberation
equally high in my esteem.
Now that I know
Śyāmā's name to be Brahman
I've stopped worrying about religion and ritual.

Rāmprasād Sen

93

Tongue, call out
"Kālī! Kālī!"
Mind, my Śyāmā Mā
sits in a six-wheeled chariot with three reins
fastened to the *mūlādhāra*.

Endowed with five powers, Her charioteer
drives Her from country to country.
Her horse
    charging ahead with the chariot
can cover ten *krośas* in a single day
  though when the chariot breaks down
  he can't even move his head.

Going on pilgrimage is a false journey, Mind;
don't be over-eager.
Bathe at Tribeni; cool yourself
in your inmost chamber.

When your body's finished, decomposing,
Prasād will be cast away.
So, Mind, seize the moment;
time is running out:
    call the Two-syllabled One
    as best you can.

Rāmprasād Sen

94

Stay within yourself, Mind;
don't go into anyone else's room.
You will get what you need right here;
search in your own inner chamber.

Cintāmaṇi is like a philosopher's stone,
that greatest treasure
able to bring countless riches:
Her front door is strewn about
with so many jewels.

Going on pilgrimage
is a journey of sorrow, Mind.
Don't be too eager.
Bathe in the three streams of bliss.
Why not be cooled at their source,
your bottommost mystic center?

What are you looking at, Kamalākānta?
This world is full of false magic.

But you fail to recognize the magician—
and She's dwelling in your own body!

Kamalākānta Bhaṭṭācārya

95

So, Mind—
you've decided to go on pilgrimage?
If you abandon the nectar of Kālī's lotus feet
you'll fall in a well
and ruin yourself.

Life is old age, sin, and disease;
these are the sufferings they offer at Puri.
Kashi—or do I mean a cough?—can kill you when you have a fever,
and bathing at Tribeni will only make your sickness worse.

Kālī's name is a powerful medicine, the best prescription:
drink it with devotion. Oh sing! Drink!
You'll become the Self, delighting in your Self!
Śiva is the Lord of Death; if you serve Him well
liberation will quickly follow.
In Him all things are possible: even you
will merge with the Supreme.

Prasād says, Brother Mind,
you've traded the shade of the wish-filling tree
for the roots of a thorn bush. Is this the way
to lose the fear of death?

Rāmprasād Sen

96

Mind, how do you think you'll find Her?
You're crazy; your house is dark!
If you have no realization,
can you catch the object of realization?
Mind, to the best of your ability
first bring yourself under control.

Otherwise, like the moon hiding at daybreak
She'll hide Herself in your small, dark room
in a secret cupboard.

I couldn't see Her
looking through the six philosophies
or the Āgamas, Nigamas, or *Tantrasāra*;
but he who appreciates the flavor of devotion
lives in that home in bliss.
Thirsting for realization, that supreme yogi
inside of you
meditates from age to age.
Once realization dawns, he'll catch hold of you
like a magnet grabbing iron.

Prasād says, I worship that yogi as the Mother.
Shall I break this pot in public?
Mind, understand through hints and gestures.

Rāmprasād Sen

97

The bee of my mind
is absorbed
in Kālī's blue lotus feet.
The honey of worldly pleasures,
the flowers like lust,
all have become meaningless.
Black feet, black bee,
black mixed with black.
Look! Happiness and suffering are now the same!
The ocean of my bliss is overflowing.

After so long
Kamalākānta's cherished hope has been fulfilled.
And see!
Those who get intoxicated by the five "m"s
seeing the fun
have beat a retreat.

Kamalākānta Bhaṭṭācārya

98

Is there any treasure like the Mother's name?
Though She's Consciousness
though She's Brahman
    if you call on Her
    She comes.

Yes, She's in the *mūlādhāra* and *sahasrāra*
but how many can know Her
by that route?
Just fall at Her feet in your heart
    and find your treasure
    right close.

You hold no lamp of knowledge in your hand?
There's no harm in that;
like a cow missing her calf,
    Mā runs to find you.

So, Mind, call out "Kālī! Kālī!";
meditate on the Mother's form.
In this way, that cloud-colored Śyāmā
    will dance, always
    dance, in your heart.

Kalyāṇkumār Mukhopādhyāy

99

Mind, you're still not rid of your illusions;
you haven't seen how Kālī is.
You know the Mother manifests
as the three worlds,
but you seem not to know it
    really.

That Mother who adorns the world
with countless jewels and gold
  aren't you ashamed to decorate Her
    with trashy tinsel?
That Mother who feeds the world

with myriad tasty treats
    aren't you ashamed to offer Her
        rice you've laid out in the sun, and
        wet chick peas?
If you really knew the Mother who
protects the world with such care,
would you sacrifice
sheep, buffalos, and young goats?

Prasād says,
Devotion is the only true way to worship Her.
You may do rituals to impress other people,
        but the Mother won't be bribed.

Rāmprasād Sen

100

Other than Your two red feet, Śyāmā,
nothing else matters.
But Tripura's Enemy, I hear, has taken them.
My courage is broken.

Family, friends, sons, wives—
in good times they're all here
but in bad times no one stays around
and my house is deserted
like the wilderness near Or village.

If You wish to rescue me,
then look at me with those compassionate eyes.
Otherwise my prayers will have
the brute force of a ghost,
useless to win You.

Kamalākānta says:
I tell my sorrows to the Mother.
My beads, my bag, my mattress—
let those stay hanging in the meditation room.

Kamalākānta Bhaṭṭācārya

101

External rituals mean nothing
when the Goddess Filled with Brahman
is roused in your heart.
If you think on the Unthinkable,
will anything else come to mind?
It's like unmarried girls
with their various amusements;
when they unite with their husbands,
where are those games?
What will you worship Her with?
Everything is full of Her essence.

And look at degenerate Kamalākānta!
She has made even him
a storehouse of good qualities.

Kamalākānta Bhaṭṭācārya

102

Mā, Hara's Beloved, Tārā,
I've heard in the Tantras that
deliverance lives in Your name.
That's why I'm always calling You—
"Tārā! Tārā! Tārā! Tārā!"
You are Tārā, Embodiment of the Three Primordial Properties,
savior of the undying world-egg.
Catching You is extremely difficult.
Tārā Mā, devotion is the only fruit of spiritual practice
that's worth anything. Kālketu, the hunter's son,
called "Durgā! Durgā!"
and got You.

I've put a tight rein on my thoughts
and purified my mind.
Tārā Mā, I've caught You,
stony girl—
there's no escaping for You now!

Tārā, today I've laid a trap for You in the garden of my heart.
The Destructive Lord Himself
told me that the teacher's mantra is a net
that I should lay out
across the path of practice—
                    and then wait awhile.
In my hand I've got the rope of devotion, too,
so if You come this way
I'll nab You red-handed
and tie You up by the feet.

I'll keep You
ever so carefully
in the prison of my heart.

People worship You in various ways—some
with a full sixteen-item ritual!
But where will I get the money for that?
Tārā Mā, falling at Your feet, with hands
cupped full, I'll offer You pure water
from the Ganges
                    and all the other offerings too
          but in my mind.
Where would I get anything else to give—
buffalos, or goats? Instead You'll get a human
sacrifice, the six enemies
          say I, shouting "Durgā!"

Mā, there's no way You can escape,
no means, no secret exit.
I repeated "Tārā," and I got You.
Now, my sinful eyes are closed
and I've employed knowledge
to guard them forever.

Mā, who can fathom Your play?
By what delusion
do You take what shapes?
Even if I give You
   oh with so many pains
gifts of money, food, or jewels,
You won't be satisfied.
Lanka's Rāvaṇa made such an effort to worship You,
but he went the way of his fathers.
On the other hand, You were pleased with Śrīmanta
who gave You no worship

and went fearlessly to the burning grounds.
Yet You rescued *him*!

Mā, You are the highest of all possible treasures.
He who worships You as such
gets You
so Vyāsa attests in the Purāṇas.

Nīlmaṇi Pāṭunī

103

I'll worship You with tears, Mā;
why do I need Ganges water?
With flames from the fire of my suffering
I'll cleanse the altar of my heart.
Day by day I'll offer You the oblations of my pain
calling "Mā!"
my mantra
while egotism and envy sizzle in the blaze.
The five senses and their objects
the six enemies—
I'll even add in my wishes and desires—
these are the gifts I place at Your feet.

So, Mā, come and stay awhile,
Wild-Haired One.
I reach out to You,
cupped hands brimming full
with the flowers of love's devotion.

Gaṇapati Pāṭhak

The Experience of *Kuṇḍalinī* Yoga

Learning to visualize the interior landscape of the body according to the meditation prescriptions of *kuṇḍalinī* yoga is an extremely complicated and arduous process that requires instruction by a teacher, memorization, and guided practice. Indeed, although Tantric practitioners laud their path as the best means to spiritual realization, Tantric texts and some of the Śākta poems contain warnings regarding impetuous aspirants who try to rouse the dormant snake without sufficient training. One must be taught how to raise the sleeping *kuṇḍalinī* and then how to control her; in addition, as one ascends from the *mūlādhāra* to the *sahasrāra*, one must remember what to expect in each of the lotuses: their shape, color, number of petals, inscribed letters, associated elements, reigning deities, vehicular animals, and characteristic mantras (see Figs. 1 and 3). Because the whole microcosmic system is so complex, and because its description reads like a series of lists, very few poets attempt to catalog it in poetic verse. Rāmprasād, however, wrote two such compositions, one of which opens the present section.

Of the upper *cakras*, three are most important. (1) The heart lotus (*anāhata*)—or, in other texts, a small lotus called the *ānanda-kanda* right below it—is especially revered because it is here that the devotee installs the image of the chosen deity for adoration and meditation, imagining her seated or dancing on an altar of jewels beneath a wish-filling tree. (2) The main image associated with the *ājñā* lotus between the eyebrows is that of the Tribeni bathing spot, where the three *nāḍīs*—*iḍā*, *piṅgalā*, and *suṣumnā*—come together in a plait, excellent for spiritual refreshment. (3) Most attention, however, is given to the *sahasrāra* at the top of the head. In whichever way it is conceived, whether as the garden of bliss where the two lovesick swans meet and unite, or a bridal chamber, or the most splendid of cities, or the tip of the Caḍak pole in Śiva's annual festival, or the minaret at the apex of the city, or the secret room reachable only through a secret passageway to the top of the nine-gated house, or the top of the stringed instrument of the body, this is the supremely desired end of the journey. For it is here that the soul, or *jīva*, which has made the journey with the *kuṇḍalinī*, experiences the absence of darkness, symbolized by the never-waning full moon. He also enjoys the supreme culinary reward: tasting the nectar that flows down from the love-play of Śiva and Śakti in the *sahasrāra*. This ambrosia is so powerful that he appears drunk to outsiders, who censure him unfairly. Finally, with the dissolution of all physical elements and mental desires, the soul, like the *kuṇḍalinī*, merges with Śiva, until it is time for the descent back through the body to the *mūlādhāra*.

In spite of the appealing and daring nature of some of the poems represented here, very few poets in the entire Śākta Padāvalī corpus, over the course of 250 years, have chosen to write on *kuṇḍalinī* yoga. In some ways this is surprising; most poets in the genre have followed the leads of Rāmprasād and Kamalākānta quite scrupulously, in terms of both content and style, and these two progenitors devoted roughly 13 percent of their outputs to this Tantric theme. What happened? Why is there such little material on the Goddess as the Serpent Power? I think the answer lies in the difficulty of the practice. Apart from a few Tantic practitioners like Rāmprasād Sen, Kamalākānta Bhaṭṭācārya, Mahendranāth Bhaṭṭācārya, and Dīnrām, authors in the Śākta Padāvalī genre have become overwhelmingly oriented toward devotion. Historically, however, Tantra has been foundational to the literary tradition, and even now a few hardy practitioners prove that Kālī the Goddess of their hearts is also Kālī the Traveler within the spiritual channels of their bodies.

104

Kulakuṇḍalinī, Goddess Full of Brahman, Tārā—
You are inside me.
You are inside me, Mā
    in the *mūlādhāra*, the *sahasrāra*,
        and the wish-granting *maṇipura*.
The Ganges flows to the left, the Yamuna to the right;
in their midst streams the Sarasvati
            where Śiva and Śakti shine.
Meditating on You like this
        a ruby-red snake sleeping
        coiled around the Lord Self-Born
a man is blessed.

In each glorious lotus
    mūlādhāra, *svādhiṣṭhāna*, *maṇipura* at the navel,
    anāhata, and *viśuddha*
You incarnate as letters
    v to s, b to l, ḍ to ph, k to ṭh,
        sixteen vowels at the throat,
            and h and kṣ between the eyebrows.
My teacher was firm with me;
he told me to think of You like this in my body.

Brahmā and the four gods, and Ḍākinī and her five *śakti*s
inhabit the ascending lotuses, supported underneath
by an elephant, a crocodile, a ram, an antelope, and a second elephant.
If you hold your breath
you can know Her
and hear the buzzing hum
of a drunken bee.
Earth, water, fire, and air dissolve immediately
when you sound "yaṃ," "raṃ," "laṃ," "haṃ," and "hauṃ."

Then cast me
a compassionate glance—
I keep bring reborn!
Your feet alone drip nectar.
You are Śakti, cosmic sound,
and Śiva the dot in "Oṃ"
full of nectar like the moon.
Who can cleave the One Self?

Ritual worship, controversies over dualism and nondualism
these don't bother me,
for the Great Mistress of Time tramples Time.
Once sleep is broken
there's no more sleep, and the soul
will be turned into Śiva. Could one like this
even if reborn
drown anew in the senses?
Liberation adores him like a daughter.

Pierce the *ājñā cakra*;
dispel the devotee's despair.
Traveling past lotuses
four, six, ten, twelve, sixteen, and two
to the thousand-petaled flower at the top of the head
the female swan unites with Her handsome mate
in the residence of the Lord.
Hearing Prasād's words,
the yogi floats in a sea of bliss.

Rāmprasād Sen

105

Screening its face amongst lotus stalks
the golden bird
contented
limbs listless with love
eyes open
sleeps on the flower with v, ś, ṣ, and s
emblazoned on its petals.

In a flower bud above
reigns the mantra "raṃ."
Repeat "raṃ! raṃ!"
and fan the flames red;
surround the swan with heat.
Let no obstacle stand in your way;
get to work—
you are young and fresh.
Break this fake sleep and snap out of your dreams;
then the storms of this world won't concern you.

Oh soul, whip up the wind; let the bird fly
flower to flower
towards Her mate in the *sahasrāra*.
When that happens the five elements in you
earth, water, fire, wind, and ether
will dissolve, and you'll be free
to merge in the Supreme.

Mahendranāth Bhaṭṭācārya

106

Who is that Śyāmā woman
standing on Bhava?
All Her modesty gone,
She plays with Him
overturning sexual custom
by being on top.
Choked up,
waves of bliss sweeping over Her,

She hangs Her head and smiles—
Love incarnate!
The Yamuna, the heavenly Ganges, and between them
the honorable Sarasvati—
bathing at their confluence
confers great merit.
Here the new moon devours the blue moon,
like wind extinguishing fire.

Poet Rāmprasād says,
Brahman is merely the radiance of Brahmamayī.
Stare at Her
and all your sins and pains
will vanish.

Rāmprasād Sen

107

Renunciation's agonies
form the stalk
where black lotuses bloom.
In the lake of my heart
streams Śakti in constant waves.
Because of this beauty
my blind darkness is lightened,
my deepest sorrows destroyed.
Through a cavity in my heart
the fiery serpent rises
blazing high. My sky brightens,
I float in breezes of bliss.
Good fortune is here; the granter of dreams
 the black moon
smiles. How can I speak of Her elegant beauty?
Colorless and yet glowing with color
Śiva's Beloved laughs in Her bridal chamber
 Dīnrām's heart.

Dīnrām

108

Meditate on Kālī! Why be anxious?
The night of delusion is over; it's almost dawn.
The sun is rising, dispelling
thick nets of darkness, and lotuses are blooming
          thanks to Śivā
at the top of your head.
The Vedas throw dust in your eyes; blind too
the six philosophies. If even the planets
can't fathom Her
who will break up these fun and games?
There are no lessons between teacher and student
in a market of bliss.
Since She owns the actors, the stage, and the play itself
who can grasp the truth of the drama?
          A valiant devotee who knows the essence—he
          enters that city.
Rāmprasād says, My delusion is broken;
who can bundle up fire?

Rāmprasād Sen

109

My Mind,
what sort of intelligence is this?
You never learned to catch a serpent,
and now you wander
in search of tricks!
A hunter's son kills birds,
a fisher's son catches fish.
Oh Mind, if the snake charmer's son is a fool
will the snake spare him?
Playing with snakes is your caste duty;
don't despise those mantras.
Mind, when your father asks you to catch a snake,
you'll hang your head in shame.
You got a treasure

but lost it through negligence.
What fool would reach for anything else?

Prasād says,
I won't lose it;
while there's still time,
I'll learn.

Rāmprasād Sen

110

Managing the house is a big problem.
The master of the house
is completely undisciplined;
he does whatever he pleases.
To him everything seems gross.

This house is attacked at its nine dread gates;
because of them I
constantly flail about.

The housewife always sleeps; day and night
She never rises. It's not just tiredness,
either. That female conspires
with Her man.

Prasād says,
If you don't shake that snake
who will wake Her up?
But once you wake Her
She'll start biting—
causing total panic.

Rāmprasād Sen

111

Everyone's flocking to Gājan
boys and girls, men and women
parading new clothes

over fields, into fairs.
Some go 'round fasting, scorched by the terrible sun,
while others stroll happily eating!
What can I say?
They're boors all—
jumping in herds
onto mats, into hopes,
roaming life to life
punctured
by nails of illusion.
With strong ropes of karma
they tie themselves up to the treetop of Being
and swing.
But at length
the day ends, the fun stops;
for the pleasures of Caḍak
last only three days
until death.

Premik says,
Renouncer! brother!
You've haven't sampled the real Caḍak.
It brings peace, not illusion,
even in an illusory world.
But in order to get it
devotion and reason are musts.

Be your own kind of renouncer;
day and night speak this truth.
Since everyone says Gājan is ruined
by too many renouncers
stay at home.
What use are other people?
How many can you invite inside?

Even if you've never used it,
the scaffolding for the jump
has been there since your birth.
So make up your mind; climb up
and jump down
but gently and secretly!
Pierce those lotuses
with the darts of your serpent missile.

Again, why not sport in the house of bliss?
Spin yourself from the thousand-tipped Caḍak tree.

If you take this type of whirl, at your end
you'll cook death.

Mahendranāth Bhaṭṭācārya

112

O Bābā! Look at this Caḍak tree.
I scale it step by step; how many more there are
I have no idea. The guru says, "It must be done;
you must climb all those stairs.
Then, child, you'll see
the Lord
dancing in a Muslim minaret."
My guru is a first-rate teacher
but his words stop my heart.
Mā, I love You so much
my body doesn't work; my knees
knock together as I climb.
What will happen, Mā? Step by step
will I make it to the top?
Or will I sprain my feet trying?

Dīnrām is besotted with love for You, Mā;
he's in no hurry.
Throw down the rope of Your mercy;
let me tie it around my waist.
Then, whether I climb
or dangle suspended,
what You do is up to You.

Dīnrām

113

You can't catch the thief, Mind,
and it's a big problem
because he's leading you into danger.
He's hiding with his friends
in the dense forest of earthly enjoyments.
That treasure you got with such effort?

He'll steal it
and embarrass you.
Other thieves steal after the householder has gone to sleep,
but this one has funny habits:
the first thing he does
is to wake the householder up!
In that house there is a room
with nine holes facing nine ways.
Inside is so much splendor
that whether or not he finds them open,
he enters.
But if you travel the secret path,
you'll be able to catch that thief.
And in this dilapidated house
make devotion your watchman
at the nine doors.

Mahendranāth Bhaṭṭācārya

114

Tell me, what are you doing now, Mind,
sitting there with a blind eye?
There's someone in your own house
but you're so oblivious
you've never noticed!
There's a secret path
with a small room at the end—
and what an amazing sight inside:
caskets filled with jewels
that you never even knew about.
There's a lot of coming and going along that path.
Go, upstairs, to the highest room,
and you'll see the moon rising.

Premik says excitedly,
Keep your eyes open;
if you want to be awake in yoga
you must travel this secret way.

Mahendranāth Bhaṭṭācārya

115

You've enchanted the world
World-Bewitcher
strumming Your vina from Your lotus, *mūlādhāra*.
Your instrument's the body, Your three strings
the *suṣumnā* and the like; with Your bowstring
the great mantra
You make music in each scale.

Bhairab raga reverberates in the lowest center,
Śrī in the lotus of six petals, *Mallār* in the *maṇipura cakra*
and *Basanta* in the heart.
In the *viśuddha cakra* one hears the swinging *Hillol* raga, while
Kānāḍā plays in the *ājñā*.
Rhythm, measure, tone, melody—
all in three octaves.

Great Illusion, how easily
You bind us in bonds of ignorance.
But when all elements are dissolved in the spiritual heights
Your lightning movements cease.

Śrī Nandakumār says, I'm still so full of doubt.
But it's You
the three primordial properties
who blocks my access
to that woman's face.

Mahārāja Nandakumār Rāy

116

Wake up, wake up, Mother!
Kulakuṇḍalinī,
how long have You been asleep in the *mūlādhāra*?
Do Your appointed *sādhana*; let's go to Lord Śiva
in the thousand-petaled lotus in the head.
Pierce those six centers, Śaṅkarī; soothe my tormented mind.

Don't worry about the channels *iḍā*, *piṅgalā*, and *suṣumnā*;
Brahmā, Viṣṇu, Mahādeva: all the gods

always meditate on You, Śivā,
and now they await You.
Visit Svādhiṣṭhāna City; come on, Crusher of Cares—
then let's go where jewels are as plentiful as thought,
and after that where the soul dwells, burning bright
day and night
    a candle flame.
The next center is *viśuddha*,
a shining lotus of sixteen petals, where Śākinī
the goddess of the region
resides in an ethereal lake.
Oh Kuṇḍalinī, then go further
to the *ājñā cakra* of two petals.

Stop at all six centers, Sarvāṇī;
manage Dāśarathi's *sādhana* for him.

Dāśarathi Rāy

117

Being the child of a Mad Mother
kills me with shame.
People around me blame me;
how can I respond?
    In fear of them
    I hide the Mother;
    I place Her carefully, secretly
    on the throne of my heart.
There the eternal play of the Loony One
continues day and night.
She dances on my heart's stage—
swirling hair and naked limb.

They'll never recognize my Mad Mother.
Bits of straw
drifting with the current in the river of life,
they're unable to float upstream.
    But Mind, if they don't learn this upside-down practice
    they'll fall into madness themselves
    and drown.

Dīnrām observes politely:
Mā is never frightful;
that Lunatic who appears in my meditation—
She is the Queen of the Three Worlds.

Dīnrām

118

Hey, it's not wine I drink
but nectar—
"Victory to Kālī!"
Winos think I'm drunk,
but my intoxication is mental.
With the molasses given by the teacher,
the spice of desire,
and my knowledge as a brewer,
the drops get distilled in a vat.
Sipping that
makes me drunk.
I purify the process with "Tārā Mā,"
the best mantra.

Rāmprasād says,
Drink this nectar
and all human aims are yours.

Rāmprasād Sen

119

Mind, don't be duped by others' sneers.
They call you drunkard? Let them.
It's not wine I love
but nectar. Today my mind the drunk
is drunk, but drunks say
I'm drunk on drink.

Day and night sit at the feet of Śiva's queen.
If you don't
        and swallow the wine of the deadly senses

you'll fall under the influence;
your head will spin.
The cosmic egg itself
            filled with yantras and pierced with mantras
floats in that ambrosial water.
She saves us all
            Tantrics and non-Tantrics
so don't leave your path because of what others say.

Some believe the three strands birth all:
            Goodness gives us righteousness
            Ignorance feelings
            and Activity deeds.
They're deluded, Mind.

If you get drunk the conventional way
you'll fall out of beat, and the Out-of-Beat Goddess of Death
            will take you on Her lap.
Rāmprasād says, If
at your final hour
you've abandoned this path
you'll be shut out.

Rāmprasād Sen

120

I've gone mad drinking nectar.
My eyes nod, my feet
stagger on my journey
through the path of knowledge.
What ceaseless wandering! But the virtuous
can tell the difference between good and bad.
I reach the source
where nectar flows in streams
and drink, eyes closed,
all my hopes fulfilled.

Here's a drunk, all are drunks.
Brother, if you get those six drunk too
they'll forget about enjoyments
and detach forever—
            the drink is that powerful.
So play with nectar; within two days

you'll renounce automatically.
Appetites can't last
with curbed senses.

What a factory this world is, brother!
Not knowing the difference between nectar and wine
everybody gets soused, acts up;
so many are drunk on the job!

The truest drunks were Gaur and Nitāi;
drinking nectar made them mad.
Feeling overcome with bliss
they mesmerized the world.

Now new drunks have joined the old;
in heaven and earth all are drunk—
stricken by the world
on account of wine
    what a lot of senseless bunk!

Mahendranāth Bhaṭṭācārya

121

From the time of the womb
a fire burns;
    come, Mind, let's sit at Kālī's feast.
I am hungry for nectar,
    always in search of it.
The flame of my appetite burns;
look at all those delicacies of love
daubed with sandalwood paste
and arranged in layers
on the platter of devotion!

To the right of my tongue stands one woman,
    another to my left;
through austerities involving these two channels
the *kuṇḍalinī* awakes.
In the lap of darkness, on the empty path
    among the lotuses in the body
Dīnrām the bee
delights in drinking that honey.

Dīnrām

In Defiance of Death

Death as a personified state has appeared several times in this anthology, although, up until now, in poems whose main subjects have been other things.[25] Such poems have expressed the fear of dying; the concern to die a spiritual death, with a clean conscience and the name of the Death-Destroying Goddess on one's lips; and the occasional sense of victory over Death, where the poets speak of smearing soot on, or disgracing, it by the strength of their devotion to Kālī.

The poems in this section deal more explicitly with the topic, either addressing Death directly or making the experience of dying the central theme. Note the progression of ideas from the poems of Rāmprasād and Nabīncandra, in which they defy Death, to those of the three twentieth-century composers. Mahendranāth shares the sense of victory over Death, but within the real-life context of his mother's cremation; Tāpas Rāy introduces the voice of Death itself, who speaks back to the poet; and Najrul Islām claims that Death is none other than the Goddess Herself.

122

This time, Kālī,
I'm going to eat You up.
I'll eat You,
I'll eat You,
Oh Compassionate to the Poor.
I was born under an evil star
and sons born then
devour their mothers.
Either You eat me
or I eat You:
we must decide on one.

I'll make a curry of Your demons and witches
and boil into a soup
with spices and ghee

the heads from Your necklace.
Your blackness I'll smear all over
my hands, my face, and my limbs.
When Death comes
I'll blacken his face too.

I say I'll eat You up
but You won't fill my stomach;
I'll sit You on my heart-lotus
and worship You mentally.
They may tell me
if I eat Kālī
I'll get into trouble with Death,
but why should I fear him?
I'll shout "Kālī!"
and stick my thumb in his face.
I'll make sure he understands
Śrī Rāmprasād is Kālī's son.
I'll cause my death myself
through mantra repetition.

Rāmprasād Sen

123

Wait a minute, Death,
let me shout to my Mother.
Let's see whether She shows up
in my hour of need.
Eventually you'll get me; why worry about it now?
It's not for nothing that I keep Tārā's name
in an amulet at my neck.
Maheśvarī is my queen, and I
a tenant in Her personal estate.
Sometimes I'm poor, sometimes rich, but I'm never late with the rent.
Prasād says, Such is Mother's play; can anyone understand it?
How can I get to the bottom of it
when even the Three-Eyed Lord could not?

Rāmprasād Sen

124

Death, get out of here!
What can you do to me?
I've got Śyāmā Mā in prison.
I've bound Her feet with mental chains
and put Her in my heart's jail.
There the lotus bloomed;
now I'm fixed on the *sahasrāra.*
My whole life I've offered
to Kulakuṇḍalinī Śakti's feet.

I've constructed such a fortress
that even if She tries
She can't escape!
Devotion, my footman,
stands guard in front, and
I've got two eyes
patrolling the doors.

Knowing that I'd get a terrible fever
I made prior arrangements:
I've drunk the tonic that brings fever down—
the words of my teacher.

Śrī Rāmprasād says,
I've broken your hold.
I'm ready
"Kālī! Kālī! Kālī!"
to start my journey.

Rāmprasād Sen

125

Can you claim to win,
Death, in a heart where lives
the Wild-Haired Goddess of the Burning Grounds?
I'll say "Kālī Kālī" as much as I like;
you can't do a thing to stop me.
I'll proclaim Her name in public
with a kettledrum; that'll keep

the fear of death away.
When your man comes to get me
I'll show him the letter that Kālī signed.
As soon as he gets the gist
he'll turn around without a sound.

Twice-born Nabīn is Kālī's son.
You're my Mother, Mā;
don't become my enemy.
I'll sit in Your lap.
Can anyone move me?

Nabīncandra Cakrabartī

126

Mā, are you really dead?
Did you breathe your last, saying "Kālī"?
Mā, with your "Kālī Kālī!"
you smeared Death's face with soot.
You didn't flinch, but easily crossed
the sea of this world.
Taking a natural and corruptible form,
you came to earth to play,
your past deeds binding you to good fortune.
But now in the stream of time
that play is over, and you have floated
blissfully into the Being
of the Blissful One Herself.

Premik says, Oh Mā—
you have merged with my Śyāmā Mā;
so clap your hands in bliss!

Mahendranāth Bhaṭṭācārya

127

Wait a moment, Death;
let me sing aloud to the Mother

and grace my eyes
with the sight of Her red feet.

The Great Lord Himself, Forgetful Śiva,
lies at my Mother's feet,
    She the Greatest Power
        the universe
        moving and still.
That's why I drape myself
in Kālī's name, printed
on a cloth.

Death replies,
Oh devoted one, does Mā belong to you alone?
I am also the Mother's child.
But where to get Her vision?
Today I wish the same as you:
        to rest in Her embrace.

Tāpas Rāy

128

Śyāmā wakes on the cremation grounds
to take Her child
at the final hour
to Her lap.
The peaceful Mother sits on the pyre
its fire hidden by Her sari of love.
        To hold him on Her lap
        She left the Kailasa of Her joy, and
        with blessings and fearlessness in Her hands
        made the cremation grounds Her home.
Why fear this place
when you'll sleep peacefully at the Mother's feet?
        Who dies ignited by the flames of this world,
        to him the Mother calls:
        "Come to My lap; come to My lap."
        To lull you to sleep, Oh Wearied by Life,
            Mā takes you to Her lap
            disguised as death.

Najrul Islām

Adoring the Daughter: *Āgamanī* and *Vijayā* Poems for Umā

In this last section we turn our attention away from Kālī and toward a much more humanized, domesticated form of the Goddess: Śiva's loyal wife Umā. Both *āgamanī* poems, which celebrate her coming, and *vijayā* poems, which lament her departure, have as their narrative context the autumnal festival or Pūjā to Durgā, with whom Umā is identified. It is a fascinating peculiarity of Bengal that there are almost no permanent temples to Durgā, a fact that partly accounts for the enormous popularity of her festival: only once a year do Bengali devotees get to gaze upon the Goddess's face. *Āgamanī* poems were originally composed to be sung as the festival neared, in anticipation of the divine visitation, whereas *vijayā* poems accompanied the rites of farewell. Even an initial reading of these poems, however, attests to the striking "mismatch" between the ritual context and its vernacular literary tradition. For not only do the poets not focus on the martial, demon-slaying Durgā but they evince mock horror when it is revealed that the precious, simple, beautiful daughter Umā is indeed Durgā and even Kālī in another form. A ten-armed Battle Queen arrives (see Fig. 4), but the Goddess longed for is a two-armed young woman, a happy wife and mother (see Fig. 5).

These poems, when strung together, tell a story. The setting is the Himalayas (supposedly somewhere in Bengal), in a city ruled over by Girirāj and his wife Menakā.[26] They have one daughter, Umā—or Gaurī or Pārvatī—whom they have had to marry off to Śiva, a thoroughly disreputable, poverty-stricken, aged, drug-addicted, homeless, two-timing, naked beggar. Figure 6 depicts a few aspects of this improper Śiva: from his half-closed eyes one can tell that he is intoxicated, and his tiger's skin cloth falls dangerously low off his waist. He lives with his wife in Kailasa, and because Girirāj and Menakā are stationary mountains, they cannot move to visit her. But they, and all of the inhabitants of their mountain city, long to see Umā, and await with passionate yearning her annual visit home. News of their daughter comes through various channels: Nārada, the matchmaker who arranged Umā's marriage; Jayā and Vijayā, the queen's maids; and the queen's own intuition, which haunts her dreams and sends her in search of astrologers and prognosticators.

The *āgamanī* poetry series usually begins with Menakā pleading with her husband to go fetch Umā from Kailasa; she accuses him of hard-heartedness and both of them for their short-sightedness in marrying their daughter to such a worthless son-in-law. Even Menakā's friends berate her for her bad judgment. Eventually the Mountain goes (or says he does) and returns on the sixth night of the Durgā Pūjā festival with Umā, who in the meantime has persuaded Śiva to let her return to her parents for a mere three days. Umā brings along her four children: Elephant-Face (Gajānana or Gaṇapati), Five-Face (Ṣoḍānana or Kārtikeya), Lakṣmī, and Sarasvatī.[27]

Menakā is deliriously happy to greet her daughter again (see Fig. 7), and sits her on her lap, as if she were a little girl, asking for news about her marital situation in Kailasa: are conditions there really as bad as she has heard? The poetry tradition is ambivalent on the answer to this question. Some poets have Umā defending Śiva, claiming that he is indeed a wealthy man and that she is happy, in spite of the presence of her co-wife the Ganges, while others portray Umā as distressed and neglected in her husband's home. At any rate, three happy days vanish quickly, and soon it is time for Śiva to come for his wife. The *vijayā* poems express the anguish of Umā's parents and friends at having to see her off again so soon; Menakā castigates both Śiva for his meanness and the ninth night of the festival for its cessation, for with the dawning of the tenth day Umā's departure is certain (Fig. 8).

Unlike the poetry centered on Kālī, these *āgamanī* and *vijayā* poems are not sung much in contemporary devotional contexts. They derive from an eighteenth- to nineteenth-century rural environment, when people had time to sit together and sing ballads that mirrored the concerns and circumstances of their lives. Indeed, many elements of late-medieval or early-modern Bengali society are reflected in these poems: child marriage to much older men; the practice among Kulīn Brahmans of marrying more than one wife; the inability of women to move freely without male accompaniment; the dependence upon matchmakers, who often force parents into unsavory choices; and the control by the husband's family over the daughter's visiting rights to her natal village.

The role of the poets in these compositions is intriguing. Because they are telling a story, they can enter into or comment on the plot in a much more creative manner than is possible in the Kālī-focused tradition. This is especially true of Kamalākānta, who in his *bhaṇitā*s watches the action, echoes what one character says to another, gives advice, and actually participates in the action. Moreover, the characters themselves refer to him, either quoting his words or asking for his company.

The overall mood of the genre, whether expressed in the story or in the *bhaṇitā*, is one of longing and loving attachment. In a sense, one might see the ritual traditions associated with Durgā Pūjā as rather male in character, with Brahman priests performing the necessary rites in Sanskrit to a Goddess who exemplifies the typically male virtues of military prowess. The Bengali poetry, on the other hand, is centered on the mother-daughter bond; most of the poems are put in Menakā's mouth, and both she and Umā are controlled by the men in their lives as to what they can or cannot do.

The poets play with this disjunction, conveying it through their portrayal of Durgā. For Umā comes as Durgā during the Pūjā; of that there is no doubt. One finds references to the worship of the nine plants and the cries made by women at auspicious times during the rituals (poem 142), as well as to the rite of *visarjana*, or immersion, when the image of the Goddess is emptied of its divine presence and consigned to the purifying waters of a river (poem 164). And yet the poets disparage attention to such ritual, exhorting instead devotion for the Goddess as daughter. They do not, in fact, want to receive Durgā into their homes at all, and claim an inability to recognize the Goddess when she arrives in her martial outfit. The situation is even more complicated and scandalous vis-à-vis Kālī. The identification of Umā with Kālī is the stuff of which Menakā's nightmares are composed, and—in a uniquely Bengali twist to the relationship between these two Goddesses—supposes that Umā became black, skeletal, and crazed because of her poverty, association with Śiva, and overall bad luck. It is the male characters, Girirāj and the poets, who remind Menakā that her daughter is Kālī, Tārā, and the universal Goddess of the Sanskrit scriptures. But she will have none of it.

Umā's identity as Durgā and Kālī, however, is not at issue for one particular poet, who combines the theme of longing for the Goddess's presence with her demon-smashing capabilities and her fame as a righter of worldly wrongs. Najrul Islām, writing during the early decades of the twentieth century when success in the independence struggle was seen to be predicated upon Hindu-Muslim and intercaste unity, called upon the Goddess to return to Bengal both to crush the British and to help eradicate prejudice. Two of his poems conclude each of the *āgamanī* and *vijayā* sections to follow.

Āgamanī

129.

Get up, get up, Mountain: no more sleep for you!
My Umā's getting big;
she needs a husband.
She's past the age for fun and games;
eight years have come and gone.
Now she's nine
and people cluck cluck
disdaining me.

Even though you understand
you pretend not to;
this is my inner pain.
Can I tell anyone
what a husband I have?
Don't stretch my patience;
just bring a man quickly;
choose someone for Umā,
and rescue her honor.

Āśutoṣ Bhaṭṭācārya

130.

Go, my Lord of the Mountains,
bring our daughter home.
After giving Gaurī away to the Naked One,
how can you sit at home
so unconcerned?
What a hard heart you have!
You know the behavior of our son-in-law—
always acting like a lunatic,
wearing a tiger's skin,
with matted locks on his head.
He not only roams the cremation ground himself,
but takes her, too!
Such is Umā's fate.
I heard Nārada say
he smears his body with funeral pyre ash.
The way he dresses is monstrous:
the garland around his neck is made of snakes!
And who would believe me—
he prefers poison to honey!
Tell me, what kind of choice is *that*?

Kamalākānta says:
Listen, Jewel of the Mountain Peaks.
Śiva's behavior is incomprehensible.
If you can,
fall at his feet and get permission to bring Umā home.
Then never send her back again.

Kamalākānta Bhaṭṭācārya

131.

Hey, Mountain King, Gaurī is sulking.
Listen to what she told Nārada in anguish—

"Mother handed me over to the Naked Lord
and now I see that she has forgotten me.
Hara's robe is a tiger's skin,

his ornaments a necklace of bones,
and a serpent is dangling in his matted hair.
The only thing he possesses is the *dhuturā* fruit!
Mother, only you would forget such things.
What's worse, there's the vexation of a co-wife
which I can't tolerate.
How much agony I've endured!
Suradhunī, adored by my husband,
is always lying on my Śaṅkara's head."

Take Kamalākānta's advice.
What she says is absolutely true.
Jewel of the Mountain Peaks,
your daughter has become a beggar,
just like her husband.

Kamalākānta Bhaṭṭācārya

132.

What a dream I had last night!
Mountain King, how long will you sleep, unconscious?
A minute ago she was standing at my head,
but now where has my Gaurī gone?
With her moon-face she called me "Mā,"
babbling like a child. Rising up in my mind
she dispelled my darkness, showering
the nectar of immortality
in her sweet, sweet words.
While unconscious, I received this treasure,
and lost it when I awoke.
I cannot bear it!

And listen to this! It's incredible—
on all sides the jackals howled,
in their midst
my Umā, alone, on the cremation ground!
Tell me, what more can I do?
Who will bring me news?
I don't know what my Gaurī is doing!

This is Kamalākānta's message,
Virtuous Queen of the Mountains.

You saw Gaurī effortlessly, dreaming in bed.
But Śaṅkara had to renounce all
for the sake of her lotus feet.
So he keeps them in his heart
with the greatest of care.

Kamalākānta Bhaṭṭācārya

133.

I got some news from Kailasa!
Oh, my God!
What are you doing, Mountain Lord?
Go, go,
go see if it's true.

Śiva has put on Umā
the burden of their household life,
while he does yoga on the cremation grounds!
Seeing him thus engaged,
people seize the chance, seize his wealth
and scatter to the winds.

Look what happened! His moon ended up
in the dome of the sky, the Ganges now
courses the earth, his snakes
live in the underworld, and his fire
endangers forests!

Umā thought so hard
about Śiva's habits
that she turned into black Kālī!
My daughter, a king's daughter,
deranged from hurt feelings!?
Now she wears strange ornaments—
completely shameless.
And this is the worst of it:
I hear she's drunk!

Īśvarcandra Gupta

134.

Bring Tārā quickly, Mountain;
I'll conceal her in my eyes.
I thought the stars in the skies
were my heart's Tārā. But now I hear
they won't send her home.

My little girl's name is Tārā
and so are the pupils in her three eyes.
She's in my heart; in order to see her
I must shut my own two eyes
streaming with tears.
Umā was the child I nursed!
She used to cry out "Mā Mā!"
Oh Mountain of Stone,
Śiva has no mother or father;
how can he understand a mother's pain?
To whom can I tell my sorrow?

Oh my golden creeper
Oh   with a face like a moon!

Andha Caṇḍī

135.

Tell me,
what can I do?
Unkind fate made me
a woman controlled and ruled by others.
Can anyone understand my mental pain?
Only the sufferer knows.
Day and night
again and again
            how much more can I plead?
The Mountain, Jewel of the Hilly Peaks,
hears but does not listen.
Whom can I tell
the way I feel for Umā?
            Who will be sad
            with my sadness?

Let the Mountain King be happy;
he has no heart.
Friend, I've decided to forget my shame.
I'll take Kamalākānta and go to Kailasa.
She's my very own daughter—
I'll fetch her myself.

Kamalākānta Bhaṭṭācārya

136.

How could you have forgotten her,
Queen of the Mountains?
She is no ordinary girl,
your golden one.
We women belong to others,
but if we don't see her, we'll die.
You're her mother;
you held her in your womb.
We watched you give her
to a naked man with matted hair.
What treasure did you see in his house
that you surrendered your daughter to him?
That stony King of the Peaks
hasn't even the slightest shame. And you—
you tied your heart with that same stone.
In birth after birth
you took difficult vows.
After great pains
you got Gaurī, the treasure.

Kamalākānta says:
You don't realize it, Queen of the Peaks,
but you have become the mother
of the three worlds'
Mother.

Kamalākānta Bhaṭṭācārya

137.

You ask me, Queen, time after time
to fetch Gaurī.
But you know very well
the nature of our son-in-law.
Even a snake can survive for a while
without its head-jewel.
But to the Trident-Bearer
Umā is more than that.
If he doesn't see her even for a moment,
he dies. He keeps her in his heart.
Why would he willingly send her to us?

Once
to win respect for the gods
Śiva drank a terrible poison.
But the pain was unbearable, and
only the shadows from Umā's limbs
could cool Śaṅkara's burning body.
Since then he has not parted from his wife.

You're just a simple woman;
you don't know how to proceed.
I will go,
but I won't say anything to the Naked Lord.
Ask Kamalākānta: see if he will go with me.
After all, she's his mother;
he may manage somehow to bring her.

Kamalākānta Bhaṭṭācārya

138.

The King of the Mountains is on his way to Hara's abode.
Feeling joy and nervous apprehension, he moves forward
sometimes quickly, sometimes haltingly.
"Today I will see Śaṅkara Śiva, and my body
will be cooled by breezes of bliss!"
At the same time he worries:

"If I can't bring her
what will I tell the Queen on my return?"

From a distance the Mountain King sees the flag of the temple,
and his body thrills with delight
as if floating in waters of love.
Still he fears: "I must not only *see* Umā,
but also bring her home."

Entering Kailasa city, the Mountain avoids Tripura's Enemy
and goes instead to the inner chambers of the house.
Seeing his daughter's face, supreme happiness
wells up; the darkness of his mind disappears.
Though the Mother of the World,
she wants to prostrate before him.
But he prevents her, taking her hands:
"Mā, your blessed feet are served by Kamalākānta.
How fortunate I am to have found you!"

Kamalākānta Bhaṭṭācārya

139.

Hey, Hara, Ganges-Holder,
promise me I can go to my father's place.

What are You brooding about?
The worlds are contained in Your fingernail,
but no one would know it,
looking at Your face.

My father, the Lord of the Mountains,
has arrived to visit You
and to take me away.
It has been so many days since I went home
and saw my mother face to face.
Ceaselessly, night and day,
how she weeps for me!
Like a thirsty *cātakī* bird, the queen stares
at the road that will bring me home.
Can't I make You understand
my mental agony at not seeing her face?
But how can I go without Your consent?

My husband, don't crack jokes;
just satisfy my desire.
Hara, let me say good-bye,
Your mind at ease.
And give me Kamalākānta as an attendant.
I assure You
we'll be back in three days.

Kamalākānta Bhaṭṭācārya

140.

I plaster myself with ashes,
twist my hair into matted locks,
and wear snakes for garlands around my neck.
He is naked, crazy, and rides a bull:
that's my husband!
I did the five austerities for five years
and got the madman of my heart.
Bowing to Him,
I laid magnolia buds at His feet.
He loves me;
the cremation-ground dweller relies on me.
Because of me
He's always floating in streams of tears.

That drug addict Bholā openly admits it:
if it weren't for me,
He'd have no one.

Giriścandra Ghoṣ

141.

Who said
if you took the name All-Destroyer
you'd be happy?
Because of the fire raging in your fate
everything has gone badly for you.
You live in a beggar's hut,
your husband always in a drunken stupor.
Ill-starred woman, you loved him so much you fed him poison.

And as for you
quaffing blood
running amuck
your good name is suspect.

He who willingly took your name
looks more dead than alive
all those ashes
smeared on his body.
No one can fathom the raging waves
of your frenzied play.
Your moon falls at your feet,
threaded bones hang on your body.
I stare at you
utterly confused.

Giriścandra Ghoṣ

142.

Consulting the omens
and considering the matter from various angles,
the Mountain Queen concludes,
"Today my Gaurī and Elephant-Face will arrive!
This is my lucky day!"

She offers a golden pitcher
smeared with sandal-flower paste
and invites Bṛhaspati
to perform the worship of the nine plants,
as is the custom.
Bewitching tom-toms and proud kettledrums
of all varieties
sound throughout the mountain city.
Women cry out excitedly:
"Ulu ulu! Ulu ulu!"

Just then
Vijayā approaches the Queen.
"Why delay any longer?
Kamalākānta's Mother, your beloved Gaurī,
has come home."

Kamalākānta Bhaṭṭācārya

143.

"How wonderful! Look what
the dawn has brought!
Your daughter's here!
Welcome her home!
Just glance at that moon-face
and your sorrow will go, scattered
like the nectar splashed
in her smile."

Hearing these splendid words, the queen
rushed out—
hair streaming, sari trailing.
Her voice was choked;
tears gushed in torrents from her eyes.
Leaving her mountain husband behind,
she fell on her daughter's neck
weeping. Then lifting her on her lap,
she gazed into that dear face
and kissed those red lips.
"Your father's a mountain,
your husband's a beggar,
and I gave you
a beautiful daughter like you
to the Naked Lord!"

All her girlfriends
overjoyed
giggled and took her by the hand:
"You didn't remember us for an entire year?
How could you forget our love?
Look at us; say something, else
we die."

Poet Rāmprasād the slave smiles
inside, floating on a great
sea of bliss. The Mother's coming
gladdens everyone. In their joy
they forget everything,
even the changing of day and night.

Rāmprasād Sen

144.

"My Umā has come!"
The Queen runs, her hair
flying every which way.

City women dash out in groups
to see Gaurī's face.
Some carry pitchers at the waist,
others hold babies to their breasts,
their hair half-braided and half-curled.
They call to each other,
"Come on! Come on!
Run quickly!
Let's go see the Daughter of the Mountain!"
Rushing outside the city,
their bodies thrill with passionate anticipation.
As soon as they glimpse that moon-face,
they kiss her lips in haste.

Then the Woman of the Mountain
takes Gaurī on her lap,
her body floating in the bliss of love.
While instruments play sweetly
heavenly musicians decorate themselves,
dancing gleefully
with the women of the mountain city.

Today Kamalākānta sees those two red feet,
and is utterly engrossed.

Kamalākānta Bhaṭṭācārya

145.

Here, Queen of the Mountains—
take your Umā;
receive Hara's life treasure.
How many entreaties I had to make!
But flattery worked on the Trident-Bearer,
and I've brought our beloved Umā home.

Now be attentive:
this is no ordinary girl, she who is worshiped
by Brahmā, Viṣṇu, and Śiva.
Śiva holds her two red feet in his heart;
he can't endure separation
even for a moment!
Your Umā is an illusion.
Infinite, yet assuming human form,
her appearance is a mere shadow.
Indeed a universe in miniature,
she takes the forms of Kālī and Tārā
to rescue the fallen, through grace.
As a reward for your endless striving, Menakā,
The Goddess Filled with Brahman
in the semblance of a daughter
calls you "Mā."

Kamalākānta says:
Blessed are you, Queen of the Mountains!
Who can describe your virtues?

Kamalākānta Bhaṭṭācārya

146.

My Gaurī,
you've come home!
Perhaps you forgot me.
It has been so long
since you called me "Mā."
A mother's heart cries night and day;
in bed, in my dreams,
I see your face.

I prayed so hard in the forest,
offering the Ganges-Bearer
flowers smeared with sandal paste,
bunches of new *bilva* leaves,
and my own fasting.
After much effort
I got my jewel.

But all the women of the mountain city make comments,
laughing and joking:

"Her husband is naked
and he lives underneath a tree!
If things were not so bad,
you'd have to wait even longer for her return!"

You are fortunate, Queen of the Mountains;
listen to Kamalākānta.
The Mother of the World, whose feet
are the treasures of Brahmā's desire—
she is your daughter.

Kamalākānta Bhaṭṭācārya

147.

"How are you faring, Umā,
at home with that beggar Hara?
I know he's crazy; what does he have for money?
He wanders from house to house begging.
Hearing of my son-in-law's state,
my chest splits with grief.

"Tārā, you are moon-faced, beautiful-eyed,
and beautifully complexioned.
I know the son-in-law's character:
there's fire on his forehead, matted hair
on his head, and he wears the bark of a tree!
I hear from others that he throws away jewels
and wears snakes instead!"

The Queen takes Gaurī on her lap
and says sweet words to her.
"My Umā, golden creeper,
Mṛtyuñjaya lives in the cremation grounds.
I die in grief over him, and also over you
and me, being separated.

"My heart laments day and night,
but since I'm a mountain woman
unable to move
I can't go see you.
Thinking over my life,
I stare in hope at the road;
I weep when I don't see you.

"Shame, shame, shame!
Is this a matter for debate?
I'm mortified every time I hear about it:
the Mountain gave you away
to a man who doesn't fear snakes
and who smears his body with ashes.

"You are all-auspiciousness,
a raft over the sea, able to ferry us
to the other side.
But when I see this suffering of yours
my grieving chest bursts;
for even you can't destroy *this* suffering."

Rām Basu

148.

The Queen asks:
"How is he, this matted-haired Śaṅkara,
Hara with the moon in his crown,
holding the trident?

"From the first time I set eyes
on the Three-Eyed Lord,
I understood him more than you.
He wears a tiger's skin,
his ornaments are garlands of bones,
and his crown is adorned with baby snakes.
His body is whiter than a silver mountain
decorated with ashes.

"But just assure me over one thing:
Tell me the real story about
your terrible co-wife, Suradhunī.
From your words I can tell that she is loved
by your husband. But how does she love you?
This is what I wonder
day and night."

Listen to Kamalākānta's words,
Queen of the Mountains.
Āśutoṣa is the crest-jewel of the gods.
He doesn't distinguish between what is his

and what is someone else's.
Whoever comes feels right at home.
Your daughter is happy.

Kamalākānta Bhaṭṭācārya

149.

From her autumn-lotus mouth
she babbles half-formed words.
Sitting on her mother's lap,
a slight smile on her blessed face,
Bhavānī speaks of the comforts of Bhava's home.

"Mother, who says Hara is poor?
His house is built of jewels more lustrous
than hundreds of suns and moons!
Since our wedding,
who has felt darkness?
Who knows when it is day or night?

"You hear that I'm afraid of my co-wife?
Suradhunī loves me more than you do!
From her perch in Śiva's matted hair
she sees how he holds me
in his heart. Who else is so lucky
to have a co-wife like her?"

Kamalākānta says:
Listen, Queen of the Mountains,
Mount Kailasa is the summit of the worlds.
If you ever saw it,
you wouldn't want to leave.
Forgetting everything,
you'd stay at Bhava's place,
Mountain Woman.

Kamalākānta Bhaṭṭācārya

150.

Get up, Mountain, get up!
Here, hold your daughter!
You see the *Caṇḍī* and teach the *Caṇḍī*,
but your own Caṇḍī has come home!
You do the auspicious ritual *maṅgalārati*
when you could be holding Maṅgalā!
Call her, wake her—
        misfortune will vanish!

I worshiped Tārā and got her,
my Tripurasundarī.
She is the sight in my eyes;
she dispels my sorrow.
        Seeing her soothes me.

Anonymous

151.

I had a good dream last night;
she came, standing at the door
        my treasured Tārā
calling "Mā! where's Mā? where's Mā?
Come to me—I'm so sad!"

I stretched out my arms
and took Umā on my lap;
I was so happy I forgot myself.

Mountain, get up;
Umā has returned to Himalaya!
Say "Victory to Durgā!" and
take her on your lap;
        "Victory to Durgā! Victory!"
One should feel love for a child;
it's not right to neglect her.
Grasping the end of my sari, Tārā asked,
"Mā, what's this? What an attitude my father has!"
        Mountain,

Pārvatī doesn't understand
            that you cannot move.

Her mother's disgrace is known the world over.
A mother's anguish
only mothers understand.
Not even a second do I get
respite from my pain.
Love binds me with chains of action.

No one can tell you anything—
you're such a stone!—but my life
drains away at people's reproach.
Where's your love? Just once
take her in your arms
and your stony self will be cleansed.

Ah, Mṛtyuñjaya won't leave
my girl for more than three days
            and ruins me.

Rām Basu

152.

Mountain,
  whose woman have you brought home to our mountain city?
This isn't my Umā;
this woman is frightening—
and she has ten arms!
Umā never fights demons
with a trident!
Why would my spotless, peaceful girl
come home dressed to kill?
My moon-faced Umā
smiles sweetly, showering nectar.
But this one causes earthquakes
with her shouts and the clattering of her weapons.
Who can recognize her?
Her hair's disheveled, and she's dressed in armor!

Rasikcandra says,
If you recognize her,

your worries will vanish.
For it's in this form
that the Mother destroys my fear of death.

Rasikcandra Rāy

153.

You're home, Umā! Stay here
please
a few days.
You've gotten so big; why such hesitation?
If you ask me to bring the son-in-law
I'll send people to Kailasa;
we'll do whatever he likes.
There's nothing crooked or insincere about him;
if you call him, he'll come.
He doesn't pout or sulk;
he's not gossipy like you.

Now I see—
you identify with that house;
that's why I'm a stranger to you.
When Hara used to come for you
you'd drown in a rush of tears.
I surrendered you into the hands of another
and now I can't tell you a thing.

Giriścandra Ghoṣ

154.

Menakā says, Hey listen, Mountain King,
when morning comes
so will the Three-Eyed God
to take our treasured Umā to Kailasa.
What to do? Speak to me!
Without Gaurī, without Umā
my sadness-chasing treasure,

I cannot live. If she leaves I'll die.
Oh Mountain King, I'm suffering;
tell me my fate.

When Śaṅkara comes to our mountain city, with what heart
will I say goodbye to Mahāmāyā? I can't forget her moon-face.
Elephant-Face, Lakṣmī, and Sarasvatī have come with her.
And look, there's Five-Face, stringing arrows on the Gāṇḍīva bow!
Satī's whole family is here—such great good fortune!
But I won't be able to bear it if she goes.
When morning comes
Tripura's Enemy will arrive.
He'll blow the horn, calling "Durgā!"
and he and she will go away.
If she forsakes Himalaya for Kailasa,
if the treasure of my austerities departs,
I'll throw myself into the sea.
When Umā is home
she calls me "Mā Mā" with her sweet voice;
life flows into my dead body. But without her
I won't be able to live in this mountain city.
See, Umā is the life of my life.

Śāradā says,
Hey, you won't be able to keep her.

Śāradā Bhāṇḍārī

155.

He who has seen my Mother
can he hate his brother?
She loves everyone in the three worlds;
her heart cries for all.
With her there's no difference of caste,
no distinction between high and low;
all are the same.
If she sees a Caṇḍāla
like Rāma with Guhak
she clasps him to her breast.
Mā is our Great Illusion, highest Nature, and
Father our highest Self;

that's why one feels love for all
we feel love for all.
If you worship the Mother
hating her children
she won't accept your *pūjā*;
the Ten-Armed One will not.
The day we forget the knowledge of difference
on that day only
will Mā come home to us.

Najrul Islām

156.

Wherever are the lowly, the suffering, and the poor
there I've seen my Mother—
my Food-Filling Mother—
though beggars' clothes she wore.
I search for Mā in heaven, taking egotism's flare,
but she comes on dusty paths
while I'm engaged in showy prayer.
Wandering wandering,
far high up in the sky,
I return to bow my head
to one of Mā's afflicted sons,
her open lap his bed.
I can't climb down to meet them,
those lowest of the low,
for whom my Mother of the World
has let all riches go.
They're hidden in a hell
of ignominy
where your blessed feet alone
willingly can be.
Take me to them, Mā; come and take me to them, Mā!

When I bring all people
to your haven of delight,
then I'll see all darkness pierced
by your resplendent light.

Najrul Islām

157.

Jayā—
don't wake up Hara's wife,
I beg you.

Because she has to leave
she stayed up the whole night crying.
All night she was in pain;
only now she sleeps.
Alas, that moon-face is grey with grief.

When she wakes
Umā will abandon us for Kailasa city,
leaving Himalaya dark.
Hara has come to take her away;
that's why I ask you to delay.

For, as long as she sleeps
I can still gaze on her moon-face.

Harināth Majumdār

158.

What happened?
The ninth night is over.
I hear the beat beat beat
of the large *ḍamaru* drums
and the sound shatters my heart.
How can I express my agony?
Look at Gaurī;
her moon-face has become so pale.
I would give that beggar Trident-Bearer
anything he asked for.
Even if he wanted my life
I'd give it up.
Who can fathom him?
He doesn't know right from wrong.
The more I think of Bhava's manners
the more stony I become.
As long as I live,

how can I send Gaurī?
Why does the Three-Eyed One crave her so needlessly?

Take Kamalākānta along
and make Hara understand:
if you don't behave honorably,
you can't expect others to treat you with honor,
either.

Kamalākānta Bhaṭṭācārya

159.

"Jayā, tell him that Umā will not be sent.

"Hara doesn't know how a mother suffers!
Whatever else you tell me
I'll agree to,
but don't tell me this.
I'll keep her in my heart
with my two eyes on guard.
Even if the Mountain says I should let her go,
I'd rather die. Gaurī's my only treasure;
she's my life. If she doesn't stay
at least three days,
I'll die of sorrow.
She's a king's daughter;
she has never known pain.
But there, with that Hara,
a beggar from birth,
she'll have so much to suffer.
He takes my treasure into the cremation grounds
and other horrible places;
he doesn't know how bad he is.
How shameless,
coming to take her away again!
Doesn't he know that she will not
be sent?"

Then Jayā answers:
"Listen, Queen of the Mountains:
I have some advice for you.
Do you realize

how many Brahmās desire the feet of that girl
you regard as your daughter?
Take Kamalākānta's humble suggestion:
'Without Śiva you won't get Śivā.
If you can,
keep your son-in-law, Śaṅkara, here.
Then your Gaurī will never leave.'"

Kamalākānta Bhaṭṭācārya

160.

Turn back, Umā,
and let me see your moon-face!
You are killing your unfortunate mother;
where are you going?

Today my jeweled palace has become dark.
What will remain in my body
but a life of ashes?

Umā, stay here!
Just for once, stay, Mā!
Cool my burning body
even for a moment.
My eyes are fixed on the road you travel.
How long must I wait
until you come home again?

Fulfill Kamalākānta's desire,
Moon-Faced One:
call your mother,
and make her understand.

Kamalākānta Bhaṭṭācārya

161.

"Hara came and made off with my Gaurī.
What are you doing, King of the Mountains,
sitting there looking so amused?

I was polite—
I tried so many ways to make him understand.
But he didn't listen; in fact,
he almost fell over with laughter.
How impossible he is:
his ornaments are snakes,
and his garment a tiger's skin
(which often slips off)!
I am the wife of a king.
How can I tolerate this?
You have thrown my golden doll into the water."

The King of the Mountains replies:
"Our son-in-law is no ordinary being;
Even the eight *siddhi*s grovel at his feet."

Kamalākānta adds, "don't worry,
Queen of the Mountain Peaks.
Send your daughter away
with the highest joy."

Kamalākānta Bhaṭṭācārya

162.

Am I afraid of the tenth day?
Go, Mā, go back home to Hara.
I'll see you off with a smiling face;
that'll make your jaw drop.
Even though you leave me in the form of Durgā,
you stay here, surrounding me,
as Kālī.
So why should I worry?
I won't try to keep you back,
clutching the end of your sari.
Just the opposite: I'm happy
knowing that Śiva will break into smiles
as the light of the full moon streams
into the darkness of Kailasa city.
The ninth day hasn't come merely to go away again;
it has come to take you.
Can you avoid it?

It has forsaken all else, Mā,
for you.

Kalyāṇkumār Mukhopādhyāy

163.

Don't go back, Mā, don't go back, Mother—
I cling to your two red feet.
You've thrown your wretched children
who went to you for refuge
on the dust of the earth.
Mā, I cling to your two red feet.
We're not immortal, neither are we gods,
but we suffer
how we suffer!
living on this earth.
We're helpless; any ability we have
comes from your compassion.
You gave your divine power to the gods
beings lacking death
but why, Mā, are you so affectionate to *them*?
The demons and the devils haven't died yet, either.
On the bosom of the earth they dance
the *tāṇḍava* in a frenzy of annihilation.

Without killing these demons first,
how can you leave us on Vijayā?

Najrul Islām

164.

Now there'll be a new mantra, Mother,
to awaken you.
You'll stay always in our homes,
your image no more dropped in river water.
The hearts of men and women of all castes—
that will be the image we worship,
Mā, the pilgrimage place where you reside.

With energy and devotion I'll install your throne there
where no high-and-low distinctions
impurity caused by touch
can be.

Everyone together
we'll speak out the Veda of Mother's name.
We're all children of one Mother—we feel it;
we'll break down walls, forget our collective injuries.
No one will be wretched, none poor; all the same—
we'll all be great India,
the Vrindavan of eternal love.

Najrul Islām

Notes

1. Śaśibhūṣaṇ Dāśgupta, *Bhārater Śakti-Sādhanā o Śākta Sāhitya* (Calcutta: Sāhitya Saṃsad, 1960), p. 207. Note that the most popular form of Kālī in Bengal is Dakṣiṇākālī, as pictured in Figure 2. Other forms of the Goddess, such as Bhadrakālī, Guhyakālī, Mahākālī, Rakṣakālī, and Śmaśānakālī, have different iconographic features. For descriptions of these, see Pratapaditya Pal, *Hindu Religion and Iconology According to the Tantrasāra* (Los Angeles: Vichitra Press, 1981), pp. 60–63.

2. In Bengali, *pūjā* is used in two senses. When written in the lower case, *pūjā* means routine ritual worship to a deity, either in a temple or at home (see note to poem 102). Durgā Pūjā, on the other hand, refers to the annual public festival of the Goddess Durgā.

3. The following historical summary is necessarily brief. Greater detail may be found in J. N. Banerjea, *Pauranic and Tantric Religion, Early Phase* (Calcutta: Calcutta University, 1966); S. C. Banerji, *Tantra in Bengal: A Study in its Origin, Development and Influence*, 2nd rev. ed. (New Delhi: Manohar, 1992); Thomas B. Coburn, *Encountering the Goddess: A Translation of the Devī-Māhātmya and a Study of Its Interpretation* (Albany: State University of New York Press, 1991); Edward C. Dimock, Jr., *The Thief of Love: Bengali Tales from Court and Village* (Chicago: University of Chicago Press, 1963); Teun Goudriaan and Sanjukta Gupta, *Hindu Tantric and Śākta Literature*, vol. 2, fasc. 2 of *A History of Indian Literature*, edited by Jan Gonda (Wiesbaden: Otto Harrassowitz, 1981); David R. Kinsley, *The Sword and the Flute. Kālī and Kṛṣṇa: Dark Visions of the Terrible and the Sublime in Hindu Mythology* (Berkeley and Los Angeles: University of California Press, 1975) and *Hindu Goddesses: Visions of the Divine Feminine in the Hindu Religious Tradition* (Berkeley and Los Angeles: University of California Press, 1986); Rachel Fell McDermott, *Mother of My Heart, Daughter of My Dreams: Kālī and Umā in the Devotional Poetry of Bengal* (New York: Oxford University Press, 2001); Malcolm McLean, *Devoted to the Goddess: The Life and Work of Ramprasad* (Albany: State University of New York Press, 1998); Carol Goldberg Salomon, "Govindadāsa's 'Kālikāmaṅgal' (The Vikramāditya and Vidyāsundara Sections): An Edition and Translation," Ph.D. dissertation, University of Pennsylvania, 1983; Sir John Woodroffe, *The Serpent Power, Being the Ṣaṭ-Cakra-Nirūpaṇa and Pādukā-Pañcaka*, 2nd ed. reprint (1918; Madras: Ganesh, 1989); and Dušan Zbavitel, *Bengali Literature*, vol. 9, fasc. 3 of *A History of Indian Literature*, edited by Jan Gonda (Wiesbaden: Otto Harrassowitz, 1976).

4. Although there are said to be thousands of arteries (*nāḍīs*) in the subtle body, three are most important: the *suṣumnā*, which travels up through the center of the spinal cord; and two others, *iḍā* and *piṅgalā*, to the left and right of it, respectively. The aspirant is taught to force his energy into the *suṣumnā* and its subsidiary inner channels, which lead him to spiritual liberation, and out of the other two, which enmesh him in attachments.

5. See Patricia Dold, "Kālī: 'Terrific' Goddess of the *Mahābhāgavata Purāṇa*," in Jeffrey J.

Kripal and Rachel Fell McDermott, eds., *Encountering Kālī: At the Margins, at the Center, in the West* (Berkeley and Los Angeles: University of California Press, forthcoming).

6. Bengali anthologies of poetry list the names of approximately 150 poets who had written on Śākta themes by the mid-nineteenth century alone. However, many of them composed only one or two lyrics, and for at least a third of them we possess no biographic information. For further discussion of these poets, see *Mother of My Heart, Daughter of My Dreams*, chapters 2–4.

7. Of the thirty-seven poets whose work is represented here, four are lost to the historian: Andha Caṇḍī, Rāmlāl Dāsdatta, Tāriṇī Debī, and Rāmkumār Nandī Majumdār.

8. These were often given the honorific titles of Kumār (Prince), Rāja (King), Mahārāja (Great King) or Mahārājādhirāja (Greatest of All Great Kings).

9. There are many more composers whose Śākta lyrics are being recorded by Bengali singers in the contemporary music market. These three have been chosen as representative because of the content and quality of their compositions. See the discography below.

10. For some possible exceptions in this anthology, see poems 65, 68, 82, 89, 100, 126, 155, 156, 163, and 164.

11. See the sections on Basavaṇṇa and Mahādēviyakka in *Speaking of Śiva*, translated with an introduction by A. K. Ramanujan (Baltimore: Penguin, 1973), pp. 61–90 and 111–142.

12. The five "m"s are five substances whose names begin with the letter "m," used in certain Tantric rites as a method of training the practitioner to experience the divine side of even the most forbidden things. They are meat (*māṃsa*), fish (*matsya*), wine (*madya*), a type of intoxicating grain (*mudrā*), and sexual intercourse (*maithuna*). Regarding the last "m," the aspirant is supposed to have ritual intercourse with a woman not his wife; she is to be thought of as Śakti, and he as Śiva.

13. There are, to be sure, scores of other Śākta poetry anthologies in Bengali, although not all of them are still in print. Some are listed below in the Notes to the Poems.

14. Fewer than a quarter of the poems in the present volume overlap those in *Śākta Padābalī*.

15. Seventeen poets, 15 percent of the total in Rāy's anthology, each of whom is represented by four or more poems, account for 195, or 60 percent, of his total collection.

16. A few others may be found in the ranks of the early- to mid-nineteenth-century entertainers, before it was considered vulgar for women to perform in public. See *Mother of My Heart, Daughter of My Dreams*, chapter 4, section "Where are Kālī's Daughters?"

17. Mahendranāth Gupta, *Gospel of Sri Ramakrishna* (Madras: Brahmavadin Office, 1907).

18. Calcutta: Oxford University Press. This contains 103 poems, the majority by Rāmprasād.

19. Jadunath Sinha, tr., *The Cult of Shakti: Ramaprosad's Devotional Songs* (Calcutta: Sinha Publishing House, 1966), and Michèle Lupsa, tr., *Chants à Kālī de Rāmprasād Sen* (Pondichery: Institut Français d'Indologie, 1967). Sinha's volume contains 313 poems attributed to Rāmprasād, and Lupsa's 123.

20. Wheaton: Quest Books.

21. Boulder: Great Eastern, 1982; 2nd ed. Prescott, Ariz.: Hohm Press, 1999. Nathan and Seely translate sixty-two of Rāmprasād's poems.

22. A much smaller collection of fourteen Śākta poems has also been translated by Sagaree Sengupta in "Poetic Visions of the Great Goddess: Tamil Nadu and Bengal," in Vidya Dehejia, ed., *Devi: The Great Goddess* (Washington, D.C.: Arthur M. Sackler Museum, 1999), pp. 107–117.

23. *Karālavadanāṃ ghorāṃ muktakeśīṃ caturbhujāṃ*, originally from the *Kālī Tantra*, quoted

by Kṛṣṇānanda Āgambāgīś in his *Bṛhat Tantrasāraḥ*, translated into Bengali by Rasikmohan Caṭṭopādhyāy (Calcutta: Nababhārat, 1982), pp. 387–388.

24. The six philosophies are Sāṃkhya, Yoga, Nyāya, Vaiśeṣika, Mīmāṃsā, and Vedānta. The Vedas are the most ancient and revered scriptures of the Hindu tradition, often called Nigamas by Tantric authors. Āgamas are frequently used as a synonym for Tantras, though as a class of texts they tend to emphasize ritual over philosophical speculation. Purāṇas are "old stories" or histories, texts filled with accounts of the worlds, the gods, and their interactions with humans.

25. The two most typical words for Death as someone to whom one can talk are Śamana and Kāla. In the translations to follow, Death is capitalized only when treated as a fellow being.

26. He is also called Girivara, Lord of the Mountains, and Śaila-Śiromaṇi, Jewel of the Mountain Peaks. Menakā's epithets include Girirāṇi, Queen of the Mountains; Śikhara-Rāṇi, Queen of the Peaks; and Bhūdhara-Ramaṇī, Mountain Woman.

27. The addition of Lakṣmī and Sarasvatī as the two daughters of Pārvatī and Śiva is a peculiarly Bengali tradition.

Notes to the Poems

The notes refer to Bengali source materials in abbreviated form, as follows:

ĀKBG	Mahendranāth Bhaṭṭācārya, *Āndul Kālī-Kīrtan o Bāul Gītābalī*, 7th ed. (1917; Calcutta: Prabodh Printers, 1987).
BŚS	Gaṇapati Pāṭhak, *Bhaktimūlak o Śyāmā Saṅgīt* (Calcutta: Maheś Library, 1968).
DĀR	Bhadreśvar Maṇḍal, *Duḥkha Āmār Raktajabā* (Calcutta: Nāth Brothers, 1988).
DRP	Dāśarathi Rāy, *Dāśarathi Rāyer Pāṃcālī*, edited by Haripad Cakrabartī (Calcutta: Calcutta University, 1962).
GG	Giriścandra Ghoṣ, *Giriś-Gītābalī*, edited by Abināścandra Gaṅgopādhyāy (Calcutta: Gurudās Caṭṭopādhyāy, 1904).
MG	Kalyāṇkumār Mukhopādhyāy, *Māyer Gān* (Calcutta: Rūpa, 1970).
NG	Najrul Islām, *Najrul-Gīti*, edited by Ābdul Ajīj Āl-Āmān, 5 vols. (Calcutta: Haraph Publishers, 1972–1975).
NP	Nīlkaṇṭha Mukhopādhyāy, *Nīlkaṇṭha Padābalī*, edited by Śaratkumār Sen (Calcutta: Śaratkumār Sen, 1904).
PKG	*Prācīn Kabioyālār Gān*, edited by Praphullacandra Pāl (Calcutta: Calcutta University, 1958).
RJR	Satyanārāyaṇ Bhaṭṭācārya, *Rāmprasād: Jībanī o Racanāsamagra* (Calcutta: Granthamelā, 1975).
SB	*Sacitra Biśvasaṅgīt*, edited by Nuṭbehārī Majumdār (Calcutta: Majumdār Press, 1910).
SGS	Dīnrām (pseud.) and Kṛṣṇa Bhaṭṭācārya, *Sādhan Gīti o Svaralipi* (Calcutta: Sāhityam, 1985).
SK	Atulcandra Mukhopādhyāy, *Sādhak Kamalākānta* (Dhaka: Ripon Library, 1925).
ŚP	*Śākta Padābalī*, edited by Amarendranāth Rāy (1942; Calcutta: Calcutta University, 1955).

ŚPŚ	Āśutoṣ Bhaṭṭācārya, *Śākta Pada Śatadal* (Calcutta: Añjan Bhaṭṭācārya, 1976).
SS	*Sādhak Saṅgīt*, compiled by Kailāscandra Siṃha, 2 parts (Calcutta: Victoria Press, 1885).
ŚS	Kamalākānta Bhaṭṭācārya, *Śyāmā Saṅgīt*, collected by Nabīncandra Bandyopādhyāy and Bipradās Tarkabāgīś Bhaṭṭācārya (Calcutta: Barddhamān Maharajadhirāja Māhtābcānd Bāhādur, 1857; reprinted 1925).
SSS	*Saṅgīt-Sār-Saṅgraha*, edited by Harimohan Mukhopādhyāy, 2 vols. (Calcutta: Aruṇoday Rāy, 1899), vol. 2.
ŚSS	Rāmreṇu Mukhopādhyāy, *Śyāmāsaṅgīt Saṅgraha* (Burdwan: Burdwan University Press, 1979).

Poem 1. *Ke o ekākinī*, *ŚP* #120. Except for the *bhaṇitā*, this descriptive list is nothing more than a Bengali translation, in slightly rearranged order, of a Kālī *dhyāna*—with the key exception that the Goddess is standing, not seated, on Śiva, and nothing is said about reversed sexual intercourse. A literal rendition of "meditate on You" in the last stanza is "do Your *dhyāna*." Bhava is a name for Śiva. Candra is Māhtābcānd's pen name. Māhtābcānd wrote similar Bengali poems on at least thirty-five goddesses whose *dhyāna*s he found in the Tantras.

Poem 2. *Kulbālā ulaṅga, tribhaṅga ki raṅga*, *RJR* #116. The Bengali translated here as standing with cocked hips is *tribhaṅga*, "one whose body has three angles [through two bends, at the knees and at the waist]." This is Kṛṣṇa's standard, erotically evocative pose. The God of Love is Kāma, or Madana, frequently said to be bewitched by Kālī's beauty.

Poem 3. *Āre ei āilo ke re ghanabaraṇī? RJR* #42. The *cakora* is a red-legged partridge, said in Hindu mythology to subsist on moonbeams.

Poem 4. *Ke raṇaraṅgiṇī*, *SSS*, p. 292. Kālī is typically accompanied by four types of female associate: terrifying spirits (*bhairavī*s), flesh-eating demons (*ḍākinī*s), fiends (*rākṣasī*s), and witches (*yoginī*s). Here she dances only with *yoginī*s. The *javā* flower is the red hibiscus, believed, because of its blood color, to be a special favorite of Kālī. The *bilva* or *bel* tree, with its greenish-grey fruit and greenish-white flowers, is sacred to both Śiva and Durgā. The point of this poem is the juxtaposition arrived at in the last line: the very Goddess whose appearance and behavior are so frightening is also Brahmamayī, She Whose Essence Is Brahman, and who is therefore beyond all attributes whatsoever. Akiñcan means Lowly One, and is Raghunāth Rāy's characteristic name for himself in his *bhaṇitā*s.

Poem 5. *Kālorūpe raṇabhūmi ālo kareche*, *ŚS* #162.

Poem 6. *Akalaṅka śaśimukhī*, *RJR* #1. The "king" (*bhūpa*) referred to here is probably Mahārāja Kṛṣṇacandra Rāy of Nadia, Rāmprasād's patron.

Poem 7. *Bhairabī bhairab jay Kālī Kālī bali*, *ŚS* #57. Brahmā is the Creator, frequently said to desire the feet of the Goddess.

Poem 8. *Bhālo preme bhulecho he*, *ŚS* #131. Śiva is Mahādeva (Great Lord), Tripurāri (Enemy of Tripura, the demons' triple city), and the Bewitcher of Madana, the God of Love.

Poem 9. *Baḍa dhum legeche hṛdi kamale*, *ĀKBG* #6. Kālī or Tārā is Bliss-Filled (Ānandamayī) and Śiva the Lord Ever-Blissful (Sadānanda). The door of knowledge could refer either to the door of Brahman (*brahmadvāra*), situated at the opening to the *suṣumnā*, the central channel of the subtle body at the base of the spine, which is the entrance and exit of the *kuṇḍalinī* in her passage to and from Śiva; or to the *brahmarandhra*, the opening at the top of the head, through which the soul, after having raised the *kuṇḍalinī* to the level of the *sahasrāra*, leaves the body in death. In Bengal it is customary at the time of death to half-emerge the dying person in the Ganges or some comparable river, so that she or he dies in contact with purifying waters. Premik, or Lover, is the name characteristically used by Bhaṭṭācārya in his signature lines. This song is often performed in public concerts by the Āndul Kālī-Kīrtan Samiti. Recorded by Maheś Rañjan Som, *Śyāmā Saṅgīt*, Gathani 4281 (1989).

Poem 10. *Ke Mā Śyāmāṅginī Mattā Mātaṅginī*, *DRP*, p. 746. The Ganges-Holder (Gaṅgādhara) is Śiva. The Kalindi River is another name for the Yamuna.

Poem 11. *Jagadambār koṭāl*, *RJR* #134. The theme of this poem is the Tantric practice of *śava-sādhana*, where the aspirant sits on a corpse (the hero's seat) in the cremation grounds and tries to retain his composure in spite of the ghosts and goblins who test his mettle by assuming hideous shapes and emitting horrible noises. Here the chief tester is the equivalent of a divine constable or policeman (*koṭāl*). The Goddess is described both as Jagadambā (the World-Mother), which emphasizes her compassion, and as Karālavadanī (She of the Grisly Face), which calls to mind her fierce qualities. By showing fearlessness in the presence of the latter, one attains the grace of the former. A mantra is a sacred utterance, in this case in praise of Kālī.

Poem 12. *Candra camke bayāne dhanya*, *SSS*, p. 52. This is one of the most explicit poems in the entire Śākta Padāvalī corpus on the connection between the zamindars' aspirations to power and their patronage of Goddess worship.

Poem 13. *Ke re pāgalīr beśe*, *ŚS* #122.

Poem 14. *O re Sarbanāśī! Mekhe eli*, *NG* 3: 303. Here the Goddess is addressed as Sarvanāśī (All-Destroyer) and Muktakeśī (Wild-Haired One). The poet also makes a pun with her name; Kāli, or Kālī with a short i, means black soot, as well as disgrace.

Poem 15. *Kāli ki tor sakali bhrānta*, *SK* #190. The fourth stanza refers to the Goddess's former life as Satī, the daughter of Dakṣa. When her father insulted her husband Śiva, she committed suicide in indignation. The poet makes a contrast between this seemly behavior toward a husband and Kālī's stance on her man's chest. Several of Śiva's epithets are used in this poem: he is Tripurāri, Paśupati (King of Living Beings), Trilocana (the Three-Eyed One), and Digambara (the Naked Lord). Likewise, Kālī is Tripurā-Sundarī (the Beautiful Goddess of Triple Nature), Kṣemaṅkarī (the Kind or Beneficent One), and Śavasana (She Whose Seat Is a Corpse). This last epithet is used sarcastically by Kamalākānta: because the Goddess has killed her husband, she really does deserve the title.

Poem 16. *Tumi kār gharer meye*, *ŚS* #14. A sari is the six yards of cloth in which Indian women dress.

Poem 17. *Śib nay Māyer padatale*, *RJR* #297. The poet refers to the "Devī-Māhātmya" section—sometimes called the *Caṇḍī*—of the *Mārkaṇḍeya Purāṇa*. However, this text says nothing at all about Kālī stepping on a demon boy who miraculously changes into Lord Śiva.

Poem 18. *O ramaṇī kālo eman rūpasī kemane?* *ŚS* #209. Women apply vermillion (*sindūra*) to their foreheads as a sign of auspiciousness. *Sattva*, *rajas*, and *tamas* are the three primordial properties, or *guṇas*: virtue, energy, and ignorance or darkness.

Poem 19. *Kāli, āju nīla kuñja*, *ŚS* #51. Although the whole poem is supposedly a description of Kālī, Kamalākānta has borrowed, at least for the second stanza, characteristics of the pacific Jagaddhātrī (Mother of the World), a form of Durgā, to beautify his portrayal. Jagaddhātrī is white-limbed, dresses in white, and wears a huge white crown and curved, birdlike earrings. *Vihaṅgī*s are small birds mentioned in folklore as telltales; *khañjana* birds are wagtails, known for their quickly flitting movements, and are used as a standard comparison for beautiful eyes in Sanskrit literature; and *tamāla*s are dark-colored trees.

Poem 20. *Anupam Śyāmārūp hyāro re man nayane, NP* #25. *Mṛdaṅga* drums are like tom-toms, and a vina is a stringed instrument, like the lyre. What is interesting about this poem is the reference to the common practice of singing "Hari-nām," or the name of Kṛṣṇa, in the context of Goddess worship.

Poem 21. *Ke jāne go Kālī keman? RJR* #117. "Oṃ" is the mystic sound or mantra that is the root of all sounds and represents the essence of Brahman. The Destructive Lord (lit. Great Time), Mahākāla, is an epithet for Śiva.

Poem 22. *Śyāmā Mā ki āmār kālo re, ŚS* #48. At the end of the first stanza, the poet is claiming that Kālī is Prakṛti (Matter), Puruṣa (Spirit), and Śūnya (Void). Recorded by Pānnālāl Bhaṭṭācārya, *Bhaktigīti*, HMV SPHO 23033 (1983); Pandit Ajay Chakraborty, *Sangitanjali*, Sagarika 31050 (1994); and Mahesh Ranjan Som, *Songs from the Kathamrita*, Ramakrishna Mission Saradapitha (1987), vol. 1.

Poem 23. *Mā āmār antare ācho, RJR* #252. The worship of the five forms (*pañcopāsanā*) refers to Sūrya, Viṣṇu, Śiva, Gaṇeśa, and Pārvatī. The last sentence of the first stanza (*Bujhe bhār dey nā se jan, tār bhār nite hā̃co*) is open to more than one interpretation. If, as translated above, one takes the Goddess as the object of *bhār deoyā*, then the line reads: "that person, who, with full understanding, refuses to burden You [with false worship], You stop to take his burdens." Here *hā̃co* means "You sneeze," and refers to a Bengali superstition: if, as one is journeying, one sneezes or hears a lizard's call, one must stop and wait. However, if the implied object of *bhār deoyā* is the person in question, who refuses to encumber himself with the burden of worshiping the Mother properly by eschewing external rituals for internal meditation, then the Goddess will refuse to help him by taking his burdens; in this case, *hā̃co* means either "You sneeze away," "avoid responsibility for," or "You sneeze" [in irritation, due to all the incense used in useless ritual worship].

Poem 24. *Mā kakhan ki raṅge thāko, ŚS* #150. The epithet Nārāyaṇī associates Kālī with Lakṣmī, wife of Viṣṇu in his cosmic aspect.

Poem 25. *Kālī hali Mā Rāsbihārī, RJR* #108. Rasavihārī, or One Who Delights in the (Circle) Dance, is an epithet for Kṛṣṇa, who charmed the cowherd girls by the side of the Yamuna River in the Vrindavan forest. Vraj is the area near Mathura where Kṛṣṇa spent his childhood.

Poem 26. *Śyāmā māyer kole caḍe, NG* 1: 210. In attempting to translate the rhyme and meter of the original, I have kept Śyām (the Bengali pronunciation of the Sanskrit Śyāma) for Kṛṣṇa, as Najrul uses this in his rhyme scheme. Although both Kṛṣṇa and Kālī are clearly necessary to Najrul's devotion, in this poem the former outshines the latter, as it is Kālī, in the capacity of *mantraguru*—that is, the teacher who imparts the sacred utterance—who points the way to Kṛṣṇa, his chosen deity, or Ṭhākur. Recorded by Anup Ghoṣāl, *Najrul Gīti*, Farida Electronics (n.d.), vol. 2; and *Kājī Najruler Abismaraṇīya Śyāmā Saṅgīt*, HMV TPHV 23030 (1988).

Poem 27. *Kālī Brahmamayī go, RJR* #101. The Goddess, though called Kālī in the first line, in her identity with Brahman transcends all names and forms. Hence even her traditional epithets—Mahākālī (Great Mistress of Time), Elokeśī (Wild-Haired One), and Digambarī (Naked One)—can be included in a list of her changing guises. She is Rāma ruling in the royal city of Ayodhya and Kṛṣṇa the cowherd lad in the pasture lands of Gokul. Jānakī and the young archer are Sītā and Rāma, heroes of the *Rāmāyaṇa*. The Ganges, Gaya, and Kashi (Varanasi) are places associated with the realization of Brahman. But all pay obeisance to Rāmprasād's Mother Whose Essence Is Brahman.

Poem 28. *Jenechi jenechi Tārā, SSS*, p. 298. Pharātarā means God; Khodā is an Arabic term for Allah; Sūrya is the Sun God; the Lord of Wealth is a reference to Kubera; Viśvakarmā, the

All-Maker, is the patron deity of builders and artists; and Badar is a Muslim saint whose name is uttered by boatmen to ensure a safe voyage. Recorded by Pānnālāl Bhaṭṭācārya, *Śyāmā Saṅgīt*, HMV HTC 2739 (1981); and Anurādhā Poḍyāl, *Māgo Ānandamayī*, Super Cassettes Industries SNCD 01/295 (1994).

Poem 29. *Tumi Brahmāṇī sei Brahmalokete, PKG*, pp. 436–437. In this poem, basically a string of descriptive affirmations—but one of the few by a woman preserved in the entire Bengali corpus—Śāradā is claiming the universality of the Goddess by seeing her in five principal ways: First, she can be the female embodiment of a male deity (Brahmāṇī of Brahmā; Rājeśvarī of Rājeśvara, or skull-bearing Śiva). In addition, she is the famed Śākta goddesses (for instance, Dakṣa's daughter Satī; Śiva's wife Pārvatī, Girirāj's daughter; and Durgā of the "Devī-Māhātmya," who kills the buffalo demon, Śumbha, and Niśumbha). Third, Śāradā shows her acquaintance with the stories of medieval Bengali narrative poems; in the *Caṇḍīmaṅgalakāvya*, Kamalekāminī is a beautiful, sixteen-year-old Goddess who appears to the merchant Śrīmanta from his ship in the middle of the sea; standing amid a cluster of lotuses, she is engaged in swallowing and then vomiting out elephants. When Śrīmanta is about to be killed in a cremation ground because of this fantastic story, which nobody believes, the Goddess Caṇḍī suddenly appears and saves him. This Goddess is also celebrated in Vaiṣṇava stories: Vimalā, a *śakti* of Lord Jagannātha at Puri; Kātyāyanī, to whom the cowherd women of Vrindavan pray so that they might obtain Kṛṣṇa as a husband; and Caṇḍī, the protectress of Rāvaṇa's Lanka, from the *Rāmāyaṇa*. Finally, she is the animating energy of significant otherworldly or religious sites (heavenly Amaravati, residence of Indra, king of the gods; the underworld hells; Gaya; Puri; Ramesvaram; Vaikuntha; and Vrindavan). Perhaps the main point of the poem is that although she assumes all these manifestations, really the Goddess is Viśveśvarī, All-Pervading, and hence cannot be defined totally by any one form or location.

Poem 30. *Baṅger ghare ghare*, sung by Amṛk Singh Arorā on *Rāṅgā Caraṇ*, Gathani 7664 (1996). This and most of Mā Bāsantī's songs are publicized only through cassette recordings, not by being printed in a book of poetry.

Poem 31. *Sakali tomār icchā, SSS*, p. 48. The Goddess's principal epithet here is Icchāmayī, She Whose Wish Is Law. In the last stanza, Tārā is equated with the yantras (mystic diagrams) and mantras found in Kṛṣṇānanda Āgambāgīś's seventeenth-century classic Tantric digest, the *Tantrasāra*. This positive portrayal of Tantra reflects the commitment of the landed gentry in the decades before and after the turn of the nineteenth century to the translation and patronage of Tantric texts. Recorded by Pānnālāl Bhaṭṭācārya, *Śyāmā Saṅgīt*, HMV HTC 2739 (1981); and Anurādhā Poḍyāl, *Māgo Ānandamayī*, Super Cassettes Industries SNCD 01/295 (1994).

Poem 32. *Man gariber ki doṣ āche? RJR* #217. Rāmprasād identifies Kālī with karma (the wheel of action), *dharma* and *adharma* (virtue and vice), *śakti*, bhakti, and *mukti* (liberation). Recorded by Dhanañjay Bhaṭṭācārya, *Śyāmā Saṅgīt*, Gathani 04027 (1987).

Poem 33. *Man gariber ki doṣ āche? ŚS* #111.

Poem 34. *Sadānandamayi Kāli, ŚS* #80. The poet here is reproaching Kālī for her playful lawlessness; as the cause of all, she is above distinctions—a fact that relativizes good and evil. Recorded by Pānnālāl Bhaṭṭācārya, *Bhaktigīti*, HMV SPHO 23033 (1983); and on *Rāmkṛṣṇāyaṇ*, HMV HTCS 02B 22802 (1982).

Poem 35. *O Mā Kālī Cirakāl-i, ĀKBG* #15. Premik here mixes awe at the Goddess's all-pervading character, sarcasm and irony at her ability to deceive, and self-denigration at his failure to rise above her jokes. This song is often performed in public concerts by the Āndul Kālī-Kīrtan Samiti. Recorded by Pānnālāl Bhaṭṭācārya, *Bhaktigīti*, HMV SPHO 23033 (1983).

Poem 36. *Ei dekho sab Māgīr khelā, RJR* #44. One can use worldly knowledge, gained through perceiving the divine with form (*saguṇa*), to break false knowledge about ultimate formlessness (*nirguṇa*). The Goddess is not at anyone's beck and call, and it is impossible to predict her actions. So one must be flexible, riding with the tide, so to speak, waiting to receive her in her own time.

Poem 37. *Ei saṃsār dhokar ṭaṭi, RJR* #45. As a whole, this poem is both celebrating the poet's perceptiveness in regard to the world and detailing his entanglement in it. A bamboo box is deceptive because one does not know what is inside it. The bazaar or store of bliss is Kālī. Once one understands how the world is constructed, as well as its underlying ephemerality, one can enjoy it and abandon oneself to the Mother's whims. In the womb, the embryo sits with his legs curled up, as if cross-legged, and is said to possess knowledge of past lives, which disappears at birth. It is possible to read the last line as sarcasm, in which case Rāmprasād is castigating the Mother for her hard-heartedness both in placing him in a world where he is bound by delusion, and in playing with him according to her own caprice.

Poem 38. *Mari go ei manoduḥkhe, RJR* #248. The Mother is referred to here as Jagadīśvarī, the (female) Supreme Lord of the World. Recorded by Pānnālāl Bhaṭṭācārya, *Śyāmā Saṅgīt*, Indian Record Company 2722–0045 (1981).

Poem 39. *Duṭo duḥkher kathā kai, RJR* #172. Although her epithet is Dayāmayī, the Compassionate, the Goddess appears to play favorites. And yet, in the end, Rāmprasād decides to trust in her grace.

Poem 40. *Tomāy balbo ki Śaṅkarī?, ĀKBG* #116. The Mother is described variously as the wife of Śiva and daughter of the mountain; as the macrocosmic World-Mother (Jagajjananī) and Queen of the Universe (Bhuvaneśvarī); and as Kālī, the giver of liberation through the practice of *kuṇḍalinī* yoga in the microcosm of the body. For *brahmarandhra*, see note to poem 9.

Poem 41. *Mā meyete khelbo putul, NG* 3: 347.

Poem 42. *Kāli sab ghucāli leṭhā, ŚS* #104. According to the legends associated with this song, Kamalākānta sings it in a cremation ground as he is lighting the funeral pyre for his first wife. In such a context, the poem reflects genuine happiness that Kālī has released him from the onerous duties of a householder, allowing him to become a renunciant. Read independently of the story, however, the song appears to taunt the Goddess sarcastically for her brand of "mercy," in which all Kamalākānta has is taken away; only in its concluding lines does he grudgingly accept her decree. The Lord (Śrīnātha) refers to Śiva. The *siddhi* plant, when ground and mixed with milk, sugar, and spices, is an intoxicating drink to which Śiva and Kālī are said to be addicted.

Poem 43. *Jay Yogendrajāyā Mahāmāyā, PKG*, pp. 284-286. All the references here are to Purāṇic stories, which Anthony uses to prove that the Goddess is not really compassionate (Dayāmayī and Karuṇāmayī). She betrays her worshipers by making them poor renouncers (note the poetic license with the stories of Brahmā, Viṣṇu, and Śiva), by ruining their happiness (Dakṣa), by dominating them (Śiva), and by abandoning them in their hour of need (Rāvaṇa in his battle with Raghunātha, or Rāma). Yogendra, or the King of Ascetics, is Śiva. Bhagavatī is the feminine of Bhagavān, or God, and is an epithet for the Goddess. *Sādhana* is spiritual practice.

Poem 44. *Ekhan ār karo nā Tārā, ŚS* #125.

Poem 45. *Cintāmayī Tārā tumi, ŚP* #170. Śambhucandra is playing on the word *cintā*, which means worry or thought. The Goddess is Cintāmayī (Full of Thought), Cintāmaṇi (the wishing gem, which becomes what one thinks), and Acintyarūpiṇī (She Who Surpasses

All Thought). On the other hand, she makes the poet worry about his problems and his food, and fails to think about his welfare.

Poem 46. *Tārā tomār ār ki mane āche? RJR* #156. This is the last of four poems traditionally said to have been sung by Rāmprasād as he waded out into the waters of the pond near his house, both to submerge Kālī's image at the conclusion of her festival and to drown himself in answer to her call. Most of the biographic accounts state that he died while singing the *bhaṇitā*. However, considering how biting and caustic this poem is—the entire composition derides the Goddess for her unfair treatment of the poet—it seems quite inappropriate as a proof text for a contented death experience. In two senses Śiva assures the devotee of the Goddess's favor: as the premier devotee, under her feet, who can vouch for her grace; and as the author of the Tantras, which point to her liberating prowess. If, without reason, one's right eye throbs, this is said to be a sign of good luck; that the poet experiences this, but gains no fortune, is part of the Goddess's deception. The last stanza is a play on Kālī's name, Dakṣiṇā. Typically this is taken to indicate the Goddess whose right foot is forward (facing the southern direction), and whose right hands offer favorable boons. But *dakṣiṇā* also means the sacrificial fee owed to one's spiritual teacher; here Rāmprasād implies that she is the sort of deity who exacts life as payment.

Poem 47. *Jāni jāni go Janani, ŚS* #158. By means of the three primordial properties or *guṇas* (*sattva, rajas*, and *tamas*), the formless *nirguṇa* Goddess becomes cognizable through form (*saguṇa*).

Poem 48. *Ye hay pāṣāṇer meye, RJR* #285. This poem shows the blending of three different aspects of the Goddess: the daughter of a stone—Umā or Pārvatī—born to the Himalaya Mountain; Kālī, who stomps on her husband and wears a skull necklace; and Durgā.

Poem 49. *Byābhārete jānā gelo, ĀKBG* #21. In this highly sarcastic poem, while chiding the Goddess for her failure to live up to her name, Annapūrṇā, Full of Food, Premik draws upon a common Bengali interpretation of Śiva's poverty and blue throat. In contrast with the Purāṇic tales, where he willingly wanders naked in the performance of his asceticism and eats poison to save the gods, in this context he is too poor to have clothes and eats the deadly mixture out of hunger, evidence of the Goddess's inability to provide for her man. Śūlapāṇi, or Trident-Bearer, is an epithet for Śiva. This song is often performed in public concerts by the Āndul Kālī-Kīrtan Samiti.

Poem 50. *Mā tor sudhā garal pān kare, SGS* #18. Whereas the poet had hoped through his worship to find the sweet Umā, or Abhayā, She Who Takes away Fear, he encounters instead Kālī in her terrifying form as Sarvanāśī and Muktakeśī.

Poem 51. *Ār chele habo nā Śyāmā, DĀR* #40. Every human suffers from three afflictions: material, spiritual, and supernatural.

Poem 52. *Tuyā anurāge āmi bhulechi pīriti, SGS* #25.

Poem 53. *Mā tui paris yadi Benārasī*, sung by Amṛk Singh Arorā on *Rāṅgā Caraṇ*, Gathani 7664 (1996). Śiva is called Bābā, or Daddy, and Bholā, or the Forgetful One.

Poem 54. *Jānilām biṣam baḍa, RJR* #141. Rāmprasād's biographers have read the reference to one lakh, or 100,000, lawyers as an indication of the number of poems the poet composed in his attempts to prove his devotion. As in poem 14 above, the last lines of the poem play on the Goddess's name Kālī, which also means blackness and disgrace.

Poem 55. *Eye baḍa biṣam leṭā, RJR* #50. The piece of land is the poet's body, which he thought he could control as he wished, so as to produce fruit fitting for devotion. But he did not bargain for the five senses, who were permitted entrance by Kālī. Rāmprasād gloats gleefully to Śambhu, or Śiva, that in order to get back at the Goddess for her deception he has cheated her of her full revenue.

Poem 56. *Śyāmā yadi hero nayane ekbār, ŚS* #43. Here the Goddess is depicted principally as Patitapāvanī, She Who Rescues the Fallen.

Poem 57. *Tāi Tārā tomāy ḍāki, SB*, p. 233. Bhavānī means Wife of Bhava, or Śiva. I have been able to find no information as to Tāriṇī Debī's background or dates, although, since *Sacitra Biśvasaṅgīt* was published in 1910, she must be from the nineteenth century.

Poem 58. *Ebār dekhbo Śib keman kore, PKG*, pp. 2–3. Raghunāth enumerates four reasons why he should be optimistic about winning Kālī's feet from Śiva: the fact that other sons have beaten their fathers (Lava and Kuśa, Rāma's sons reared by their mother Sītā at the forest hermitage of Vālmīki, the author of the *Rāmāyaṇa,* conquered their father in battle); the strength of his devotion and austerities; his martial prowess as the son of Kālī and Śiva, both warriors; and Śiva's legendary generosity (for instance, in helping Aśvatthāmā of the *Mahābhārata* to avenge the murder of his father Droṇa by giving him a divine dagger). This poem is full of epithets for both Śiva and Kālī. The former is called Trilocana and Bholā, and the latter Brahmamayī, Durgatiharā (Destroyer of Obstacles), Hara-Aṅganā (Wife of Hara), Ādyāśakti (Primal Power), Muktidātrī (Emancipation-Giver), Jagaddhātrī, Jaganmātā (Mother of the World), Śailasutā (Daughter of the Mountain), Paramātmārūpiṇī (She Whose Form Is the Supreme Soul), and Brahmasanātanī (Eternal Brahman).

Poem 59. *Anna de Mā Annapūrṇā, SSS*, p. 51. Here the Goddess is called Annadā (Food-Giver), Annapūrṇā (Full of Food), Śāradā (the Goddess Who Comes in Autumn—i.e., Durgā), Jñānadā (Knowledge-Giver), and Mokṣadā (Freedom-Giver). Annapūrṇā is said to dwell with Śiva in Kashi.

Poem 60. *Patita pābanī parā, RJR* #181.

Poem 61. *Apār saṃsār nāhi pārāpār, RJR* #5. Recorded by Pānnālāl Bhaṭṭācārya, *Śyāmā Saṅgīt*, HMV HTC 2739 (1981); and Anurādhā Poḍyāl, *Māgo Ānandamayī*, Super Cassettes Industries SNCD 01/295 (1994).

Poem 62. *Tārā mā yadi keśe dhore, ŚS* #116.

Poem 63. *Doṣ kāro nay go Mā, DRP*, p. 748. The unceasing flow of devotion's tears may reverse the flooding waters of time, which have ruined the plot of land, a cipher for the poet's body. The Goddess is Kālamanorāmā (She Who Delights the Heart of Time [Death or Śiva]), Triguṇadhāriṇī (Embodiment of the Three Guṇas, or Primordial Properties), and Kṣemāṅkarī. Recorded by Pānnālāl Bhaṭṭācārya, *Śyāmā Saṅgīt*, HMV HTC 2739 (1981); and Anurādhā Poḍyāl, *Māgo Ānandamayī*, Super Cassettes Industries SNCD 01/295 (1994).

Poem 64. *Tor khātire loker khātir, SGS* #14.

Poem 65. *Āmāy deo Mā tabildāri, RJR* #14. This poem is stated by Rāmprasād's biographers to have been the first composition to draw others' attention to his talent. Employed as a clerk in an accountant's office in Calcutta, he was doodling in his spare time, writing poetry in his ledger. Upon learning of this, his boss was so impressed with the quality of his artistry that he sent him home with a stipend to continue his literary pursuits. The association of this poem with this story is based upon the image of the treasurer, or accountant. Rāmprasād is critiquing both Śiva and Kālī: Śiva, for supposedly being in possession of the treasure of the Goddess's feet, holding them on his chest, but in fact giving them away to other devotees; and Kālī, for entrusting such a lazy steward with the job. As Ardhanārīśvara, Śiva Half Woman, he is responsible for only half his body. The Goddess's father, through her identification with Umā, is the hard-hearted Himalaya Mountain, whereas the poet's father is generous Śiva. Recorded by Dhanañjay Bhaṭṭācārya, *Ḍub de re man Kālī bale: Bhaktigīti*, Hindusthan Records 2722—C375 (1989); and Maheś Rañjan Som, *Rāmprasādī Bhaktigīti*, HMV TPHVS 842532 (1994).

Poem 66. *Keman kare tarābe Tārā, ŚS* #142.

Poem 67. *Śmaśān bhālobāsis bale, ŚP* #224. The Goddess is Śyāmā and Śmaśānavāsinī (Dweller on the Burning Grounds), and Śiva is Mṛtyuñjaya (Conqueror of Death) and Mahākāla. The poet plays on similarities between the words for heart, mind, or thought (*citta*) and funeral pyre (*citā*). Recorded by Dhanañjay Bhaṭṭācārya, *Śyāmā Saṅgīt*, Gathani 04027 (n.d.); and Śrīkumār Caṭṭopādhyāy, *Kicchu Nāi Saṃsārer Mājhe: Śyāmā Saṅgīt*, CBS Inc. (1991) and *Ār Kono Sādh Nāi Mā: Śyāmā Saṅgīt*, HMV FPHVS 843110 (1998).

Poem 68. *Jāgo Śyāmā jāgo Śyāmā, NG* 3: 316. Najrul interprets Kālī's traditional cremation ground imagery in a novel way, linking it to the events of British domination in the 1920s and 1930s, when Indians needed nourishment and nerve to achieve Independence.

Poem 69. *Calo man sudarbāre, SS*, part 2, p. 110. Rāmdulāl (d. 1851) was the Dewān of Tripura, and presumably wrote this poem out of his own experience.

Poem 70. *Man re kṛṣi kāj jāno nā, RJR* #238. Recorded by Dhanañjay Bhaṭṭācārya, *Man re Kṛṣi Kāj Jāno Nā: Bāṅglā Chāyāchabir Bhaktimūlak Gān*, HMV STHV 824299 (1984); and Anup Jāloṭā, *Man Calo Nija Niketane*, Music India 4227 976 (1989).

Poem 71. *Pitṛdhaner āśā miche, RJR* #183. This poem was collected fairly late (end of the nineteenth century), and is incomplete, without a signature line. In content it is similar to poem 58, by Raghunāth Dās.

Poem 72. *Bal re jabā bal, NG* 4: 462. Recorded by Mṛṇālkānti Ghoṣ, *Kālo Meyer Pāyer Talāy: Bāṅglā Bhakti Gīti*, HMV STHV 24103 (1988); *Kājī Najruler Abismaraṇīya Śyāmā Saṅgīt*, HMV TPHV 23030 (1988); and Maheś Rañjan Som, *Śyāmā Saṅgīt*, Gathani 4281 (1989).

Poem 73. *Ebār Kālī kulāibo, RJR* #53. This poem abounds in the imagery of blackness: Kālī's name, the Black One; the poet's desire to become black like her; the black soot with which he blots Death's face; and the Goddess's inky color and disgraceful disposition, which he is reminded of every time his fingers get stained black by the juice of the world—but which he refuses to admit as an obstacle to devotion. If she is really black in color and in deed, he will recognize and celebrate her for it.

Poem 74. *O re man bali bhaja Kālī, RJR* #78. Kālī has two associations with the fifty letters: first, the necklace of fifty heads around her neck is said to represent the alphabet, each letter of which begins one of her epithets; and second, according to *kuṇḍalinī* yoga, all fifty letters are inscribed upon the first six lotuses of the subtle body, in which Kālī dwells as the serpent power (see Fig. 3).

Poem 75. *Kāj ki āmār nayan mude, ŚSS*, pp. 31–32. The poet agrees that Kālī is Muṇḍamālī (She Who Is Garlanded with Heads) and Abhayā, but not that she is Śavāsanā or Karālī (the Shocking or Terrible).

Poem 76. *Śukna taru mañjare nā, ŚS* #108. The tree is the poet's body, and the fires threatening to burn it up are the six passions or enemies.

Poem 77. *Kālī nām agni lāgilo, SSS*, p. 303. Mantra repetition not only destroys inappropriate thoughts and feelings but also inspires devotion and freedom from worldly attachments.

Poem 78. *O Mā ḍākgāḍi to chāḍbe ebār, MG* #58. The words in quotation marks are, in the original poem, English words transliterated into Bengali.

Poem 79. *Man re bhālobāso tāre, RJR* #226. This poem has no single sustained metaphor for the world, preferring instead to refer to it variously as a sea, a marketplace, a puppet show, and a divided kingdom. The last stanza refers to the *sahasrāra cakra*, where Śivā (Śiva's wife) sports with her lord on a jeweled altar under a wish-filling tree, on a jeweled island in a sea of nectar. Rāmprasād's degenerate condition can be blamed both on his own shortcomings and on the fetters placed on him by the Enchantress (Māyāvinī). But only she can free him.

Poem 80. *Kālī keman dhan khepā man, ŚS* #182.

Poem 81. *Man re tore bali āmi, ŚP* #251. The original investment is the spiritual capital one is born with; if one cannot make a profit on it or, worse, forfeits it altogether, then life has been a waste.

Poem 82. *Man, kena Māyer caraṇ chāḍā? RJR* #213. This song is always cited in the biographic literature as the proof text for a charming story about one of Kālī's appearances to the poet. One day, he was mending his fence, a job which requires two people, with his little daughter. His wife called her inside for a moment, but then she returned, and together father and daughter finished the job. Only later did Rāmprasād realize that his daughter had never left the house, and that therefore the girl who had helped him was the Goddess herself.

Poem 83. *O re man caḍaki caḍak karo, RJR* #77. Caḍak or Gājan is a Śaivite festival that occurs in March-April, at which devotees prove their devotion or fulfill a vow by various acts of bodily austerity. In the particular events referred to here, devotees are either swung around a tall pole by ropes passed through iron hooks secured in the flesh of their backs, or are encouraged to jump down from scaffolding onto mats which only thinly cover iron spikes. The point of the poem is that sexual pleasure, if properly understood, can engender spiritual insight. Seeing the parallel between touching a woman's breasts and offering *bel* leaves to two phallus-shaped Śiva lingas spiritualizes the former act. The same sentiment is expressed in the signature line, where Rāmprasād states that the inessential can give rise to the essential. However, for those without spiritual knowledge, sexuality only enslaves; the tall Caḍak pole, which causes people such hurt, is homologized to the erect phallus. The Lord of Yogis (Ascetics) is Śiva. The *khemṭā* is a jaunty, sexy dance, with much hip swaying, performed by women.

Poem 84. *Bhabe ese khelbo pāśā, RJR* #199. The old game of *pāśā* was played on a cross-shaped board (similar to that of the modern equivalent, Parcheesi). Two players moved their pawns around the board, depending on their dice throws. Each player had three dice, each with four faces; on them were one, two, five, and six holes, or dots. The highest throw, therefore, was an eighteen, and the lowest a three. Starting off the game with a five was considered a bad throw; thirteen, sixteen, and eighteen were better. Getting "stuck" in the five and six probably indicates the five senses and the six enemies. In this vein, the six and two, and the six and four, refer to the six enemies and the mind and intelligence (*man* and *buddhi*) and the same plus thought and egotism (*citta* and *ahaṃkāra*), respectively, none of which Rāmprasād can control. By one's own bad throws, in addition to an opponent's good ones, one could be made to go back to the beginning of the game—a reference to rebirth after an unfruitful life. I am grateful to Minati Kar for her sleuthing into the complexities of this now-rare game, and for her interpretation of the poem.

Poem 85. *Yadi ḍublo nā ḍubāye, RJR* #280. The word for the poet's oarsmen eyes is *Hāḍi*, a group of people now designated as Scheduled Caste.

Poem 86. *Śyāmā Māyer bhaba taraṅga, ŚS* #155.

Poem 87. *Kata ḍheu uṭheche dil dariyāy, ĀKBG* #180. The (male) body-boat is constructed of the five elements (earth, water, fire, air, and ether), and it has nine holes (two eyes, two nostrils, two ears, one mouth, and two orifices for evacuation). Note that except for the substitution of Hari for Kālī, this song could easily pass for a Śākta composition. It is frequently sung by the Āndul Kālī-Kīrtan Samiti in their public concerts.

Poem 88. *Tin Kālīr uday,* recorded by Anup Jāloṭā, *Jagat Jananī Māgo*, Atlantis AND 091 (1995). Rāṇī Rāsmaṇī financed the construction of the Daksinesvar temple and the installation of its Kālī image, called Bhavatāriṇī. Because of the Rāṇī's low-caste origins the temple has been stigmatized in some circles ever since, but because of its associations with Rāmkṛṣṇa his disciples have glorified its benefactress. Here she is portrayed as divine. So as to make his convalescence from throat cancer easier for his disciples, Rāmkṛṣṇa lived at a house at Syampukur in north Calcutta for three months in 1885, prior to being moved to the Kasipur Garden house, where in the following year he died. Śāradā Debī, Rāmkṛṣṇa's wife, endured many hardships for his sake. Once, while journeying to see her husband at the Daksinesvar temple, she had to pass through a lonely and deserted ten-mile stretch of field called Telobhelo. She was accosted by dacoits, but her simplicity and sincerity so charmed them that they cared for her and helped her on her journey, rather than robbing her.

Poem 89. *Eso bhāi sakale mile, ĀKBG* #171. This poem was written to stir up fervor against the first partition of Bengal, initiated by Lord Curzon in 1905. The Bengali protest spawned the first *svadeśī* movement, which Gandhi was later to imitate, in which Indians were urged to buy only goods made in their own country (*svadeśī*). "Victory to the Mother" is the theme song of the nationalist movement, Baṅkimcandra Caṭṭopādhyāy's famed *Vande Mātaram.* Words inside quotation marks are, in the original, English words transliterated into Bengali. A *dhuti* or dhoti is a cloth for men, wrapped over the loins and the legs and tucked in the back at the waist. This translation endeavors to follow Mahendranāth's own rhyme scheme.

Poem 90. *Kāl megh uday halo antar ambare, RJR* #94. Peacocks dance in the rain, and evoke the union of lovers. Here curved lightning flashes, like smiles, are reflected off mountain sides. The thirsty bird is the *cātaka* (fem. *cātakī*), a type of cuckoo, which is said in poetic literature to subsist on raindrops. Hence it stares at the clouds, hoping for rain.

Poem 91. *Ār bāṇijye ki bāsanā, RJR* #37. In the Tantric perspective, says the third stanza, worldly props can be used toward the ultimate goal of worldly renunciation. In the fourth stanza, Time's Door is the *brahmadvāra*, or entrance to the *suṣumnā*. Puruṣa or Nivṛti (Spirit, the male principle of cessation and renunciation) and Prakṛti or Pravṛti (Matter, the female principle of desire and activity) are yoked. From Puruṣa emanates knowledge (*vidyā*), and from Prakṛti ignorance (*avidyā*). Knowledge, in turn, gives rise to discrimination (*viveka*), which kills the cause of ignorance, or Prakṛti. Hence the grandson of Puruṣa kills Puruṣa's wife, Prakṛti. In the signature line, as a symbol of her newly married status a bride's hair parting is dabbed with vermillion powder by her husband during the wedding ceremony. Since there is traditionally no widow remarriage for upper castes, trying to place vermillion on a widow's head is not only impossible but also ridiculous, and shows a complete lack of discernment.

Poem 92. *Ebār āmi sār bhebechi, RJR* #52. Morning and evening are traditional times for ritual practice. With the advent of knowledge, however, punctuated time ceases to have meaning. In addition, reaching the *sahasrāra* is said to be such a luminous experience that it is as if there is no more night. Rubbing up gold is an analogy for bringing out the original clarity of mind. The jeweled temple is the poet's heart, which he also wants to cleanse.

Poem 93. *Kālī Kālī balo rasanā re, RJR* #97. This poem compares the body to a chariot, but makes the point that the vehicle should be used for inner, not external, pilgrimage. The six wheels are the bottom six *cakras*, from the *mūlādhāra* to the *viśuddha*, which are the five material centers, and the *ājñā cakra*, which is the abode of the mind. The three reins, or cables, are the *iḍā*, *piṅgalā*, and *suṣumnā nāḍīs*. The charioteer is the soul, or the *jīva,* and his "five powers" (*kṣamatās*) can be understood variously: as the five senses (*indriya*), the five vital forces or breaths (*prāṇa*, *apāna*, *vyāna*, *samāna*, and *udāna*), or the five *śaktis* (*kriya*, *jñāna*, *icchā*, *cit*, and *niyati*). It is also possible that the five refer to the group of five Śivas resident in the first five *cakras*. Concerning the horse of the mind, the *kuṇḍalinī*, along with the *jīva,* is said to be led upward as a rider guides a trained mare by the reins. A *krośa* is a unit of measurement equivalent to a little over two miles. The ten *krośas* are the five senses and their five objects. "Kā-lī" is the "Two-syllabled One." Recorded by Maheś Rañjan Som, *Śyāmā Saṅgīt*, Gathani 4281 (1989).

Poem 94. *Āpanāre āpani dekho*, *ŚS* #99. This poem exhorts an inner pilgrimage through the three streams of bliss (*nāḍīs*) and the stations of the *kuṇḍalinī*'s ascent from the *mūlādhāra* to the *sahasrāra*. Cintāmaṇi resides in the *anāhata* (the jeweled heart lotus). Recorded by Mahesh Ranjan Som, *Songs from the Kathamrita*, Ramakrishna Mission Saradapitha (1987), vol. 1.

Poem 95. *Man bhebecho tīrthe yābe*, *RJR* #234. This poem pits the life-giving strength of Kālī's name against the death-dealing consequences of going on pilgrimage. In stanza two, old age, sin, and disease are called "various *bhogas*"—that is, both food offerings and sufferings. Kashi means both Varanasi, the city that promises liberation to those who die there, and a cough. Aside from its meaning in the subtle physiognomy of the body (see p. 103), Tribeni is also a confluence of three actual rivers; the most celebrated occurs at Allahabad, although there is a famed one in northern Bengal, as well. The point is that swimming in cold river water when one is sick, physically or spiritually, is not likely to ameliorate one's condition. Kālī's name is the wish-filling tree; thorn bushes are external pilgrimage sites.

Poem 96. *Man karo ki tattva tāre*, *RJR* #211. An ignorant person is like a dark house: the inhabitant cannot see what lies inside. But just as the moon, though veiled by the light, is always present in the sky, or the magnet is always ready to pull iron to itself, so the inner yogi is ever waiting for realization to awaken. When it does, the house will be lighted, and the aspirant will see.

Poem 97. *Majilo āmār man bhramarā*, *ŚS* #165. For the five "m"s, see note 12 above. Recorded by Rāmkumār Caṭṭopādhyāy, *Rāṅgā Jabā Ke Dilo Tor Pāy?*, Hindusthan Records 1722–C170 (n.d.); Śrīkumār Caṭṭopādhyāy, *Kicchu Nāi Saṃsārer Mājhe: Śyāmā Saṅgīt*, CBS Inc. (1991); Anup Ghoṣāl, *Sādhanā: Bhaktigīti Saṅkalan*, Anupama Audio Cassette Co. AAC 001 (1989); and Mahesh Ranjan Som, *Songs from the Kathamrita*, Ramakrishna Mission Saradapitha (1987), vol. 1.

Poem 98. *Māyer nāmer matan dhan ki āche? MG* #21. In the first stanza, the Bengali terms employed are Caitanyarūpiṇī (She Whose Form Is Consciousness) and Brahmasvarūpiṇī (She Whose Form Is Brahman).

Poem 99. *Man tomār ei bhram gelo nā*, *RJR* #222. Recorded by Pānnālāl Bhaṭṭācārya, *Bhaktigīti*, HMV SPHO 23033 (1983).

Poem 100. *Ār kichu nāi Śyāmā Mā tor*, *ŚS* #81. This song is always quoted in the biographic literature as illustrating a seminal event in Kamalākānta's life. He was traveling alone from Kalna to Burdwan through a deserted stretch of land, and near a village named Or a group of dacoits jumped out at him, ready to rob and kill him. But he sang this song, and so melted their hearts that they not only let him go but also became his disciples.

Poem 101. *Yār antare jāgilo Brahmamayī*, *ŚS* #120.

Poem 102. *Mā Harārādhyā Tārā*, *PKG*, pp. 272–73. Kālketu the hunter is a character in the medieval Bengali narrative poem, the *Caṇḍīmaṅgalakāvya*. The Goddess Caṇḍī appears to him in the guise of a lizard, which he takes home to his wife. Thereupon the lizard becomes a beautiful woman, whom the couple recognize as a goddess. They then popularize her worship on earth. A full, sixteen-item *pūjā* consists of the following elements: (1) invoking the deity; (2) offering her a seat; (3) giving her water for her feet, (4) for her head and body, and (5) for her mouth; (6) bathing her; (7) dressing her; (8) adorning her with a sacred thread; (9) sprinkling her with perfume; (10) decorating her with flowers; (11) burning incense and (12) waving an oil lamp in front of her; (13) feeding her delicacies; (14) prostrating oneself in front of her; (15) circumambulating her; and (16) dismissing her. For Rāvaṇa and Śrīmanta, see note to poem 29. Vyāsa is a legendary sage credited with the compilation of various revered Hindu texts, such as the Vedas, the *Mahābhārata*, and the Purāṇas.

Poem 103. *Pūjbo tore aśrunīre*, *BŚS* #16.

Poem 104. *Kulakuṇḍalinī Brahmamayī*, *RJR* #113. This poem describes much of what the aspirant is supposed to visualize in the system of seven *cakra*s located in the subtle body. As a proper name, Kulakuṇḍalinī is a synonym for Kuṇḍalinī. The three *nāḍī*s are often homologized with rivers: the *iḍā* with the Ganges, the *piṅgalā* with the Yamuna, and the *suṣumnā* with the Sarasvati. At the *mūlādhāra*, the *kuṇḍalinī* lies coiled three and a half times around a self-born (*svayambhū*) Śiva linga. The *kuṇḍalinī* is said to buzz like a love-drunk bee when she is first awakened through the hot air pressed down upon her when the yogi holds his breath. The Goddess is Brahman, the savior Tārā, Śakti, Mahākālī, and the *kuṇḍalinī* herself, sometimes described as a female swan (*haṃsī*) journeying up to meet her mate (*haṃsa*). When their union occurs, the aspirant loses all sense of duality; like the Goddess, he too merges with Lord Śiva. When the mystic syllable "Oṃ" is written in Sanskrit, there is a *bindu*, or dot, at the top of the character that is said to contain the essence of all, and hence is equated with Śiva. Note that, with respect to the typical ordering of the lotuses and their contents, Rāmprasād's version has a few peculiarities: the *sahasrāra* is not mentioned until the end of the poem; sometimes Rāmprasād lists what is to be found in the first four lotuses, while at other times he includes the fifth or even sixth (for example, four elements, five males deities, five vehicular animals, and five mantras, but six female *ḍākinī*s); and he rearranges the traditional order of the mantras (compare against Fig. 3).

Poem 105. *Badan ḍheke padmanāle*, *ĀKBG* #55. The ascent of the *kuṇḍalinī* is here likened to the journey of a swan, who is aroused from her lotus-couch in the four-petaled *mūlādhāra* and incited to meet her mate in the *sahasrāra*. The serpent is said to be facing downward, her mouth over the opening to the *svayambhū* linga, which is nestled among the lotus filaments. Above the linga is the "door of Brahman," or the entrance to the *suṣumnā*. "Raṃ"of the second stanza is the fire mantra, which belongs in the *maṇipura cakra* at the navel; repeating this kindles the flame of desire, which in turn encircles and stimulates the slumbering serpent or, in this case, swan. There are three knots or obstacles that must be pierced as the *kuṇḍalinī* ascends: the Brahma-*granthi*, at the door to the *suṣumnā*; the Viṣṇu-*granthi* at the heart; and the Rudra-*granthi* between the eyebrows. Regarding the final stanza, the aspirant or individual soul (*jīvātmā* or *haṃsa*) is supposed to think of himself as *śakti* or *kuṇḍalinī* in her journey toward the Supreme Soul (*paramātmā* or *paramahaṃsa*). The identity of individual and Supreme souls is realized after the dissolution of all breaths, mental activity, and desire.

Poem 106. *Śyāmā bāmā ke birāje bhabe*, *RJR* #298. Not only is Kāma, the God of Love, bewitched by the sight of the Goddess; often she is said to embody him. As the snake of energy rises through the body, each prior state collapses or is dissolved into the next higher one. Just beyond the confluence of the three rivers at the *ājñā cakra*, above the region of the moon, lies the *nāda*, or primordial sound, in the shape of a crescent, or new moon. Hence when the aspirant raises the *kuṇḍalinī* to the level of the *ājñā*, the new moon "devours" the full moon. The parallel to wind and fire could either be a conventional analogy or it could refer to the similar process of dissolution that occurs as the wind of the *anāhata* extinguishes the fire of the *maṇipura*.

Poem 107. *Hṛdayer sarobare nityaśakti prabāhinī*, *SGS* #8.

Poem 108. *Bhābo nā Kālī bhābanā kibā*, *RJR* #201. After the aspirant has mastered the technique of raising the *kuṇḍalinī* to the height of the *ājñā cakra*, there is no further relationship between teacher and student. Spiritual liberation, gained through success in *kuṇḍalinī* yoga, sublates all other forms of knowledge, whether scriptural, philosophical, or astrological, all of which are, in any case, controlled by the playful, deceiving Goddess. Only she herself can open the gate to the *sahasrāra* by causing the lotuses to bloom, and once this occurs, the devotee will be unable to keep the realization hidden.

Poem 109. *Man re tor buddhi e ki? RJR* #240. The *ojhā* not only charms snakes but is also adept at removing their poison. The implication here is that one plays, untutored, with *kuṇḍalinī* yoga to one's cost.

Poem 110. *Ghar sāmlā biṣam leṭhā, RJR* #128. The master of the house is the *jīva*, who, due to lack of spiritual realization, lets his attention wander from object to object in an undisciplined manner and sees the world in its *sthūla*, or gross, form. This is also a hint that he has not yet awakened the *kuṇḍalinī* from her sleeping place in the *mūlādhāra*, which is said to be gross, coarse, and solid. The serpent sleeps, coiled around the Śiva linga, in the *mūlādhāra*. From the perspective of the aspirant, their sleep can be seen as a mutual conspiracy against him. When the *kuṇḍalinī* is roused—by the application of heat, air, and repetition of the mantra "haṃ!"—and enticed to make her upward journey, she pierces, or bites, each of the lotuses strung along the *suṣumnā*'s path. For an unprepared *jīva*, this can be frightening.

Poem 111. *Māṭhe hāṭe sabāi yuṭe, ĀKBG* #75. Like poem 83, this poem uses the Śaivite Gājan festival to illustrate the human condition. Not knowing the Truth but jumping onto spikes or twirling around a pole by a rope threaded through the flesh in one's back: this is a metaphor for the way people hurt themselves in vain activities. The true Caḍak tree is the central channel of the subtle body, through which the *kuṇḍalinī* climbs to the thousand-petaled *sahasrāra*, enjoys herself, and then jumps down again. The three days of the first stanza refer to the three stages of life: youth, middle age, and old age. "Too many renouncers spoil Gājan" is similar to the English "too many cooks spoil the broth."

Poem 112. *O Bābā cokh caḍakgāche, SGS* #26. Bābā means Father or Daddy, but "O Bābā" as an exclamation connotes fright or amazement. The minaret is the highest place in the city of the body, namely the *sahasrāra*.

Poem 113. *Dharte pārli nā man core, ĀKBG* #71. Here the thief is worldly desire, which makes the normal person awake with anticipation. But devotion prevents desire from entering, and the practice of *kuṇḍalinī* yoga along the secret path leads to his capture and incapacitation.

Poem 114. *Balo nā ekhan karis ki man, ĀKBG* #57.

Poem 115. *Bhuban bhulāili go Bhuban Mohinī, SSS*, p. 63. The Goddess here is both the divine musician, dwelling inside our subtle bodies, and the bewitcher of the world (Bhuvana-Mohinī) or Great Illusion (Mahāmāyā), who embodies the three *guṇa*s. Each scale, or raga, has its own associated time of day and mood: *Bhairab* is the first scale to be played in the morning after sunrise, and is soft and melancholy; *Śrī* is tender and lethargic, played as the afternoon is fading; *Mallār* is a midday scale, and connotes the rainy season, passion, and desire; and *Basanta* and *Hillol* are both springtime ragas, but whereas the former is delicate, the latter is virile and rough, like a swinging war dance. Finally, *Kānāḍā* is to be played near midnight, and evokes deep satisfaction. The three octaves in a musical composition and the three *guṇa*s are associated, respectively, with the three regions of the subtle body: the *mūlādhāra* and the *svādhiṣṭhāna cakra*s correspond to the lowest octave and *tamas*; the *maṇipura* and *anāhata* to the middle octave and *rajas*; and the *viśuddha* and *ājñā* to the highest octave and *sattva*. The three *guṇa*s are, then, integral to life and music. But, as the third stanza indicates, when realization dawns, movement of any sort, like that characteristic of lightning or that necessary to music, is completely calmed. Note that no sound of any sort is heard in the enlightened experience of the *sahasrāra*. Recorded by Anup Jāloṭā, *Man Calo Nija Niketane*, Music India 4227 976 (1989).

Poem 116. *Jāgo jāgo Janani, DRP*, pp. 748–749. Sarvāṇī means Wife of Sarva, the Universal One, Śiva.

Poem 117. *Āmi khyāpā Māyer chele haye, SGS* #19. Dīnrām's crazy Mother (Pāgalinī) is not frightful (*bhayaṅkarī*) but is the Queen of the Three Worlds (Tribhuvana-Maheśvarī). The upside-down practice is Tantra.

Poem 118. *O re surāpān karine āmi, RJR* #80. Recorded by Dhanañjay Bhaṭṭācārya, *Ḍub de re man Kālī bale: Bhaktigīti*, Hindusthan Records 2722–C375 (1989); Maheś Rañjan Som, *Rāmprasādī Bhaktigīti*, HMV TPHVS 842532 (1994); and *Rāmkṛṣṇāyaṇ*, HMV HTCS 02B 22802 (1982).

Poem 119. *Man bhulo nā kathār chale, RJR* #233. The cosmic egg (*aṇḍa*) refers both to the macrocosm, which is said to float on both wine and causal waters, and to the bodily microcosm, whose inner fluids and rivers are homologized to nectar. In either case, Rāmprasād is arguing that what he drinks is sacred and life-giving, as it sustains both the universe and the body. If one takes the second meaning as primary, then the yantras could be understood as the seven lotuses or *cakras*, which are pierced by mantras as the aspirant moves the serpent power up through the spinal column. Regarding the identity of those whom the Goddess is saving in the last sentence of stanza two, one could either translate *kula* and *akula* as "the decent" (belonging to the family) and "the disreputable" (those outside matrimonial limits), or read them as "those belonging to the Kula or left-handed Tantric path" and "those outside the Kula path." However one interprets the language, the poet is urging himself not to abandon his community. In the third stanza, the three strands, or *guṇa*s, are intoxicants; for one who is spiritually sober, they have no power to effect any transformation at all. Vaitālī as a name of the Goddess has a double entendre: she is the patron of those who sing out of beat (and hence are confused), and she is the mistress of ghosts. In other words, attachment to the world results only in death. Recorded by Rāmkumār Caṭṭopādhyāy, *Śyāmā Saṅgīt*, EMI HTCS 02B 2597 (1985).

Poem 120. *Āmār man meteche sudhāpane, ĀKBG* #51. Gaur and Nitāi are Caitanya and his chief friend, Nityānanda. Note the blending of Śākta and Vaiṣṇava imagery: the nectar comes from Śiva and Śakti in union at the end of the path of knowledge, but the exemplars of divine drunkenness are Vaiṣṇava.

Poem 121. *Prāṇjaṭhare agni jvale, SGS* #10.

Poem 122. *Ebār Kālī tomāy khābo, RJR* #54. In some versions, stanzas two and three are reversed. It is preferable to cause one's own death, if one has the spiritual power to do so, than to be caught unprepared. Recorded by Dhanañjay Bhaṭṭācārya, *Ḍub de re man Kālī bale: Bhaktigīti*, Hindusthan Records 2722–C375 (1989); and *Rāmkṛṣṇāyaṇ*, HMV HTCS 02B 22802 (1982).

Poem 123. *Tilek dāḍā O re Śaman, RJR* #158. In legends depicting Rāmprasād's life, he is said to sing this song either as his friend and patron, Mahārāja Kṛṣṇacandra Rāy, is dying, or as he himself is preparing for death at the hands of murderous dacoits. Recorded by Dhanañjay Bhaṭṭācārya, *Ḍub de re man Kālī bale: Bhaktigīti*, Hindusthan Records 2722—C375 (1989).

Poem 124. *Tui yā re ki karbi Śaman, RJR* #159. The fever is the delirium brought about by attachment to the world, which prevents adequate preparation for death.

Poem 125. *Bhay ki Śaman tore, ŚP* #285.

Poem 126. *Mā ki maraṇ marili?, ĀKBG* #138. Mahendranāth apparently composed this when his mother's body was burning on the funeral pyre.

Poem 127. *Ekṭu dā̃ḍā O re Śaman*, sung by Amṛk Singh Arorā on *Trinayanī*, Gathani 7551 (1995).

Poem 128. *Śmaśāne jāgiche Śyāmā, NG* 5: 129. Recorded on *Kājī Najruler Abhismaraṇīya Śyāmā Sangīt*, HMV TPHV 23030 (1988).

Poem 129. O*ṭho oṭho Giri tumi ghumāye theko nā ār, ŚPŚ* #1, p. 9.

Poem 130. Y*āo Giribara he, āno yeye nandinī, ŚS* #215. Gaurī means fair or golden- complexioned. In contrast to poem 49 above, here Śiva's proclivity for poison is part of his ornery disposition. Recorded by Amar Pāl, *Jāgo he Ei Nagarbāsī: Bhaktigīti*, HMV TPHVS 28116 (1987).

Poem 131. *O he Girirāj, Gaurī abhimān kareche, ŚS* #216. The *dhuturā* fruit is the white thorn apple, which yields a powerful narcotic. Suradhunī, or Divine River, is an epithet for the Ganges.

Poem 132. *Āmi ki herilām niśi svapne, ŚS* #217.

Poem 133. *Kailās-saṃbād śune, ŚP* #17.

Poem 134. *Āno Tārā tvarāy Giri, ŚP* #23. This poem, by a woman about whom nothing is known, is a play on the word Tārā, which means Savior (an epithet for Umā); pupil (in the eye); star; and the third person plural pronoun, they.

Poem 135. *Balo āmi ki karibo, ŚS* #219.

Poem 136. *Tā̃re keman pāsare rayecho, ŚS* #220.

Poem 137. *Bāre bāre kaho Rāṇi, ŚS* #222. Here we get a third twist to the poison theme (see notes to poems 49 and 130): Śiva drank the poison, as the Purāṇic tales would have it, but survived only because of the ministrations of Umā.

Poem 138. *Girirāj gaman karilo Harapure, ŚS* #223.

Poem 139. *O he Hara Gaṅgādhar, ŚS* #225. For *cātakī*, see note to poem 90.

Poem 140. *Āmi bhasma mākhi jaṭā rākhi, GG*, p. 259. The five austerities (*pañcatāpa*) involve five fires: the blazing sun overhead and four huge fires kindled at each of the four directions.

Poem 141. *Ke bale re Sarbanāśī nām nile, GG*, p. 257. Śiva is the one who took her name and has ended up under her feet, nearly dead. "Moon" here is an affectionate term for a lover.

Poem 142. *Girirāṇī yantra-sādhan mantra paṛe, ŚS* #226. Bṛhaspati is the priest of the gods. The nine plants always worshiped in conjunction with Durgā, who is said to embody them, are: two types of arum, ashoka, banana, paddy, pomegranate, sesbania, turmeric, and wood apple. The "Ulu ulu" cry is made by women at auspicious occasions, such as weddings and the annual festivals of deities.

Poem 143. *Āj śubhaniśi pohālo tomār, RJR* #1, p. 212 (*āgamanī* section).

Poem 144. *Āmār Umā elo bale Rāṇī elokeśe dhvy, ŚS* #232.

Poem 145. *Girirāṇi, ei nāo tomār Umāre, ŚS* #233. Recorded by Amar Pāl, *Jāgo he Ei Nagarbāsī: Bhaktigīti*, HMV TPHVS 28116 (1987).

Poem 146. *Elye Gauri! bhabane āmār, ŚS* #235.

Poem 147. *Kao dekhi Umā, keman chile Mā, SSS*, p. 247. Mṛtyuñjaya, or Conqueror of Death, is an epithet for Śiva.

Poem 148. *Rāṇī bale jaṭil Śaṅkar, ŚS* #238. Āśutoṣa, One Who Is Easily Pleased, is another name for Śiva.

Poem 149. *Śarat-kamal-mukhe, ŚS* #236.

Poem 150. *Gā tolo gā tolo Giri, ŚP* #72. Caṇḍī is both the name of a revered text (see note to poem 17) and the name of the Goddess Umā or Durgā. *Maṅgalārati* is the ceremonial waving of lights in front of the deity at dawn, precisely the time of day when Umā, also called Maṅgalā, the Auspicious, returns on the seventh day of the Durgā Pūjā. Her coming banishes all that is unfortunate and inauspicious (*amaṅgala*).

Poem 151. *Gata niśiyoge āmi he dekhechi susvapan, PKG,* pp. 161–162.

Poem 152. *Giri, kār kaṇṭhahār ānile Giri-pure?, ŚP* #41. Note the same "who is this?" motif that opens many of the battlefield poems.

Poem 153. *Esechis Mā thāk nā Umā, GG,* p. 364. Recorded by Rāmkumār Caṭṭopādhyāy, *Eto Gaynā Beṭi Kothāy Peli? Bhaktigīti,* Hindusthan Records 1722–C376 (1989).

Poem 154. *Menakā kay he śuno, PKG,* pp. 437-438. The Gāṇḍīva is a mythological bow said to have been used by Arjuna, one of the five heroes of the *Mahābhārata,* in battle.

Poem 155. *Māke āmār dekheche ke, NG* 1: 198. Guhak was a lowly hunter who accompanied Rāma to the forest as his servant, thus illustrating the Lord's grace. Najrul calls the Goddess Mahāmāyā and Prakṛti, and Śiva Paramātmā; if they are our parents, then all—high and low, Hindu and Muslim, men and women—must unite in love to make Bengal a fitting place for the Goddess's presence.

Poem 156. *Dīner hate dīn, NG* 5: 91. The rhyme and meter of the translation attempt to mirror that of the original.

Poem 157. *Jāgāyo nā Hara-Jāyāy, ŚP* #93.

Poem 158. *Ki halo, nabamī niśi hailo abasān go, ŚS* #241. The *ḍamaru* is a tabour shaped like an hourglass.

Poem 159. *Jayā balo go pāṭhāno habe nā, ŚS* #243.

Poem 160. *Phire cāo go Umā, ŚS* #245. In the third stanza, Mā is used as a diminutive, for a little girl.

Poem 161. *Āmār Gaurīre laye yāy Hara āsiye, ŚS* #244. The eight *siddhi*s, or powers, gained through yogic mastery, are the abilities: to make one's body small; to make oneself very light; to enlarge one's body; to get whatever one wishes from far away; to fulfill one's desires; to charm anyone at will; to control or rule over anyone at will; and to bring into being anyone or anything one desires.

Poem 162. *Daśamīke bhay ki āmār?, MG* #52.

Poem 163. *Yās ne Mā phire, yās ne Jananī, NG* 4: 317. The composer notes that this is a pained petition of an earth child, written for a short drama on the theme of Vijayā. The demons and the devils are the British, who dance the *tāṇḍava,* Śiva's dance of destruction, in India. Recorded by *Kājī Najruler Abismaraṇīya Śyāmā Saṅgīt,* HMV TPHV 23030 (1988).

Poem 164. *Ebār nabīn mantra habe, NG* 4: 259. Vrindavan, where Kṛṣṇa sported with the cowherd women, connotes passion and idyllic harmony between people united by love to one deity.

A Guide to Selected Names, Terms, and Texts

āgamanī: Songs sung in anticipation of Umā's once-yearly visit to her parents, Girirāj and Menakā, at the commencement of the autumnal Durgā Pūjā festivities.

Āgamas: A class of ritual texts that are equated in the Śākta poetry with the Tantras.

ājñā: One of the seven *cakras*, located between the eyebrows. Visualized as a lotus with two petals, it is here that the three principal *nāḍīs* or energy channels come together, like a confluence of rivers.

anāhata: The *cakra* situated in the heart, at the center of which is an altar of jewels beneath a wish-filling tree. This is said to be the ideal place to install one's chosen deity for adoration and meditation.

Āndul Kālī-Kīrtan Samiti: The Andul Society for Kālī Songs, founded in 1885 by Premik, or Mahendranāth Bhaṭṭācārya (1843–1908), for the perpetuation of his devotional compositions to Kālī. The Samiti is still performing, and enjoys a wide reputation in Calcutta.

Annapūrṇā: She Who Is Full of Food, an epithet for Pārvatī or Umā. As an appellation in the Śākta poetry, Annapūrṇā can occur in a context of either petition or sarcasm—in the latter case, the poet castigates the Goddess for his hunger pains.

Bābā: Father or Daddy, an epithet for Śiva, who, as the Goddess's husband, is the poets' father.

bhakti: Devotion, an attitude of love and intimacy toward the divine. Bhakti was expressed in poetry to male deities such as Viṣṇu and Śiva from as early as the ninth century in south India, but did not touch and transform Kālī and Umā in Bengal until the mid-eighteenth century.

bhaṇitā: The signature line at the end of a poem into which the author inserts his name, either to comment on what he has written or to incorporate himself into the action of the narrative.

Bhava: An epithet for Śiva derived from the word for "world" or "universe."

Bholā: The Forgetful One, a name for Śiva that indicates his often inebriated, self-absorbed nature.

bilva or *bel*: A type of tree with greenish-grey fruit and greenish-white flowers that is considered sacred to both Śiva and Durgā.

Brahmā: The Creator, who, along with Viṣṇu and Śiva, is frequently said to be unable to grasp the Goddess's essence, although he ardently desires her feet.

brahmadvāra: The door of Brahman situated at the opening to the *suṣumnā*, the central channel of the subtle body at the base of the spine, that is the entrance and exit of the *kuṇḍalinī* in her passage to and from Śiva.

Brahmamayī: She Whose Essence Is Brahman, an epithet for Kālī.

Brahman: The eternal, absolute ground of being, that which transcends all opposites and all language. Brahman is regularly identified with Kālī in the Śākta poetry.

Caḍak: A Śaivite festival that occurs in March-April, at which devotees prove their devotion or fulfill a vow by various acts of bodily austerity, such as being swung around a tall pole by ropes passed through iron hooks secured in the flesh of their backs, or jumping down from scaffolding onto iron spikes.

cakora: A red-legged partridge believed to subsist on moonbeams.

cakras: The seven power centers of the subtle body through which the *kuṇḍalinī* passes on her journey from her home at the base of the spine to her trysting place with Śiva at the top of the head.

Caṇḍa: One of the two demon generals whom Kālī decapitates in the third story of the "Devī-Māhātmya." See entry under Muṇḍa.

Caṇḍī/Caṇḍī: The *Caṇḍī* is a popular Bengali term for the "Devī-Māhātmya" text. As an epithet, Caṇḍī refers to several forms of the Goddess: for example, the deity to whom Rāvaṇa prays in the Sanskrit *Rāmāyaṇa*, and the beautiful divine heroine of the Bengali *Caṇḍīmaṅgalakāvya*.

Caṇḍikā: Another name for Ambikā or Durgā, from the "Devī-Māhātmya."

Caṇḍīmaṅgalakāvya: one of the medieval Bengali *maṅgalakāvya*s, or narrative poems in praise of the auspicious character of a particular deity. The *Caṇḍīmaṅgalakāvya* celebrates Caṇḍī, who is both a form of Pārvatī and an independent goddess who offers salvation.

cātaka/ī: A type of cuckoo said in poetic literature to drink nothing but raindrops.

Cintāmaṇi: An epithet for the Goddess derived from the word for "wishing gem."

*ḍākinī*s: Flesh-eating demons, one of the four types of female beings who typically accompany Kālī.

Dakṣa: The father of Satī, famous for causing his daughter to commit suicide in indignation over his failure to invite her husband Śiva to a grand sacrifice he was sponsoring for the gods.

Dakṣiṇākālī: The most popular form of Kālī in Bengal. Her right (*dakṣiṇa*) foot is forward (facing the southern direction), and her right hands offer boons.

Daksinesvar Temple: The Kālī temple in northern Calcutta associated with the Śākta saint Rāmkṛṣṇa and his wife Śāradā Debī.

Dayāmayī: The Compassionate, an epithet for Kālī.

"Devī-Māhātmya": The "Glorification of the Goddess," three stories collected in the sixth century and inserted into the *Mārkaṇḍeya Purāṇa*. The second story, about Durgā or Caṇḍikā defeating Mahiṣa, the buffalo demon, is the most famous. The third is important in the history of Kālī, who springs forth from Durgā to help slay three demons, Caṇḍa, Muṇḍa, and Raktavīja; this constitutes Kālī's debut in Purāṇic literature.

*dewān*s: Financial managers of the landed estates belonging to important aristocratic families in eighteenth- and nineteenth-century Bengal. Many *dewān*s composed Śākta poems in their spare time.

dhyāna: Tantric description of a deity used as an aid to her mental construction and installation in the heart, for the purpose of meditation.

Digambara/Digambarī: The Naked One, referring either to Śiva or to Kālī.

Durgā: The martial, ten-armed goddess who is acclaimed in the "Devī-Māhātmya" for her killing of the buffalo demon Mahiṣa. She is also said to be a form of Umā and hence the wife of Śiva, though in her form as demon slayer Śiva is typically absent.

Durgā Pūjā: The annual festival to Durgā, which occurs in September/October and which celebrates her victory over Mahiṣa. Aside from the Sanskrit worship of the Goddess based on the "Devī-Māhātmya," the Pūjā also occasions the performance of Bengali *āgamanī* and *vijayā* songs, addressed to the Goddess in her form as Umā.

five "m"s: Five substances whose names begin with the letter "m," used in certain Tantric rites as a method of training the practitioner to experience the divine side of even the most forbidden things. They are meat (*māṃsa*), fish (*matsya*), wine (*madya*), a type of intoxicating grain (*mudrā*), and sexual intercourse (*maithuna*) with a partner not one's spouse. Sometimes these five "m"s are to be conceived literally; more often, symbolic substitutes are employed.

Gājan: Another name for the Śaivite Caḍak festival.

Gaurī: The Fair One; Umā or Pārvatī.

Girirāj: King of the Mountains, an epithet for Umā's father, the Himalaya Mountains.

Girirāṇi: Queen of the Mountains, an epithet for Umā's mother, Menakā.

guṇas: Three primordial properties or strands in all living and material things—*sattva* (virtue), *rajas* (energy), and *tamas* (ignorance or darkness).

guru: A spiritual teacher and guide.

haṃsa/ī: The *kuṇḍalinī* is sometimes described as a female swan (*haṃsī*) journeying up to meet her mate (*haṃsa*). When their union occurs, the aspirant loses all sense of duality; like the Goddess, he too merges with Lord Śiva.

Hara: The Destroyer, an epithet for Śiva.

Hari: Common Bengali name for Kṛṣṇa.

iḍā: One of the three principal arteries or channels (*nāḍīs*) in the subtle body, running to the left of the spinal cord.

Jagaddhātrī: Mother of the World, a form of Durgā.

javā: The red hibiscus flower, believed, because of its blood color, to be a special favorite of Kālī.

Jayā and Vijayā: Menakā's two attendants in the *āgamanī* and *vijayā* poetry, whose chief function is to announce to the Queen that her daughter Umā has returned home.

jīva: The individual soul, said to make the upward journey through the spiritual body as or with the *kuṇḍalinī*.

Kailasa: Śiva's mountain home, where he lives with Umā.

Kāla: Time or Death; sometimes an epithet for Śiva.

Kālī: The Mistress of Time or Death; the feminine form of Kāla and hence the consort of Śiva.

Kālketu: A hunter in the medieval Bengali narrative poem, the *Caṇḍīmaṅgalakāvya*, who helps popularize the worship of the Goddess Caṇḍī.

Kashi: The name by which Śiva's holy city of Varanasi (Banaras) is usually referred to in the Śākta poetry and its associated lore.

Kṛṣṇa: The Black One, the irresistible cowherd lad described in Purāṇic prose and devotional poetry who beguiles the Vraj cowherd women—especially Rādhā, his favorite—with his flute.

Kṛṣṇānanda Āgambāgīś: Author of the popular seventeenth-century classic Tantric digest, the *Tantrasāra*, in which may be found many of the *dhyāna*s employed by the Bengali Śākta poets.

Kṣemaṅkarī: The Kind or Beneficent One, an epithet for Kālī.

Kubera: The Lord of Wealth.

Kulakuṇḍalinī: A synonym for Kuṇḍalinī, used as a proper name, frequently for Kālī.

kuṇḍalinī yoga: A Tantric spiritual practice wherein the skilled aspirant learns to raise his spiritual energy, coiled as a female serpent (*kuṇḍalinī*) in the base of his spine, up through the six centers or *cakras* in the central channel of his body to the seventh and last center at the top of his head. There the *kuṇḍalinī* unites with her consort, Śiva, bringing the aspirant to non-dual liberation.

linga: The phallus-shaped symbol of Śiva.

Mā: Mother

Madana: The God of Love, also called Kāma, who is said in the Śākta poetry tradition to be enchanted by Kālī.

Mahādeva: Great Lord, an epithet of Śiva.

Mahākāla: The Destructive Lord (lit. Great Time), another of Śiva's epithets.

Mahākālī: Great Mistress of Time, a name for Kālī.

Mahāmāyā: Great Illusion, a designation for Kālī.

Mahārāja: Great King, an honorific title bestowed upon a wealthy, loyal zamindar—in the seventeenth and early eighteenth centuries by a local Mughal representative, and in the eighteenth to mid-twentieth centuries by the British.

Mahārājādhirāja: Greatest of all Great Kings, similar to but even grander than Mahārāja.

Maheśvarī: Queen, an epithet for Kālī.

Maṅgalakāvya literature: The medieval Bengali genre of long narrative poems celebrating the exploits of various deities, among whom are numerous goddesses including Kālī and Umā.

maṇipura: The third *cakra* of the subtle body, situated at the navel.

mantra: A mystic sound or sacred utterance to be repeated in meditation as a means of spiritual advancement.

Menakā: Umā's mother.

Mṛtyuñjaya: Conqueror of Death, an epithet for Śiva.

Muktakeśī: Wild-Haired One, an epithet for Kālī.

mūlādhāra: The lowest of the seven *cakras* in the subtle body, located at the base of the spine, where the *kuṇḍalinī* lies coiled as a female serpent.

Muṇḍa: With Caṇḍa, the two demon generals whom Kālī decapitates in the third story of the "Devī-Māhātmya."

nāḍī: Artery or energy conduit within the subtle body, of which there are said to be thousands. The three most important are the *iḍā*, *piṅgalā*, and *suṣumnā*.

Nārada: The match-maker who arranged Umā's marriage to Śiva, and who continues as a go-between, carrying messages from Umā in Kailasa to her mother Menakā in the Himalayas.

Nigamas: A name often used by Tantric authors to indicate the Vedas. In the Śākta poetry, Nigamas are frequently classed with Āgamas as texts which cannot confer salvation.

nirguṇa: Lit. without qualities, usually used to describe the formless Brahman, which transcends attributes altogether; the opposite of *saguṇa*, with which it is usually paired.

"Oṃ": The mystic sound or mantra that is the root of all sounds and represents the essence of Brahman.

Pārvatī: Daughter of the Himalaya Mountain; Śiva's wife Umā.

piṅgalā: One of the three principal arteries or channels (*nāḍīs*) of the subtle body, running to the right of the spinal cord.

Prakṛti: Matter, the female principle of desire and activity, said to cause ignorance and delusion. See also entry under Puruṣa.

prati-vātsalya bhāva: The affection that a child feels toward his or her mother; the characteristic mood of the Kālī-centered bhakti poetry.

Premik: Lover, the pen-name used by Mahendranāth Bhaṭṭācārya (1843–1908) in his poetry *bhaṇitās*.

pūjā: Daily ritual worship to a deity, either in a temple or at home, in which the deity is honored as a guest, with flowers, food, water, incense, bell-ringing, and the waving of lights.

Purāṇas: A genre of Sanskrit "old stories" or histories spanning the fifth to the eighteenth centuries that are filled with accounts of the worlds, the gods, and their interactions with humans.

Puruṣa: Spirit, the male principle of cessation and renunciation that gives rise to knowledge and discrimination. Puruṣa and Prakṛti, when joined together, create the universe.

Rādhā: The cowherd woman most beloved by Kṛṣṇa; descriptions of her beguiling appearance are regularly borrowed by the Śākta poets to beautify Kālī.

Rāja: King, an honorific title given to a zamindar for loyal service. See Mahārāja.

Raktavīja: Lit. Blood-Drops, the name of a self-replenishing demon in the third story of the "Devī-Māhātmya," whom Kālī kills by licking up all his blood, so that none can fall to the ground and become a new demon.

Rāma: The hero of the Sanskrit epic, the *Rāmāyaṇa*, who kills Rāvaṇa, demon lord of Lanka, to avenge the kidnapping of Rāma's wife Sītā.

Rāmkṛṣṇa: Bengali saint and devotee of Kālī who until his death in 1886 was the chief priest of Daksinesvar, the Kālī temple in northern Calcutta. His example of love for the Goddess has rendered him one of the most revered Bengalis of the last century; some admirers even claim that he was an incarnation of Kālī.

Rāvaṇa: The anti-hero of the *Rāmāyaṇa*, whose lust and pride compel him to snatch Sītā from Rāma, an act that eventually results in his death. The Śākta poets have a soft spot in their hearts for Rāvaṇa, as Caṇḍī, or Kālī, is supposedly the patron goddess of his city Lanka. The fact that she let him down by allowing him to be conquered by Rāma is cause for their sympathy.

sādhana: Spiritual practice.

saguṇa: Lit. with qualities, typically stated of the divine with form; the opposite of *nirguṇa*, with which it is frequently paired.

ṣahasrāra: The highest and most important *cakra*, depicted as a thousand-petaled lotus at the top of the head where the *kuṇḍalinī* unites with Śiva.

Śākta: (As an adjective) emphasizing or devoted to Śakti in one of her forms; (as a noun) a person who considers the worship of Śakti to be his or her primary mode of approaching the divine.

Śākta Padāvalī: Collected Poems to the Goddess, a genre of poetry focused on Kālī and Umā that has been composed in Bengal since the late eighteenth century.

śakti/Śakti: As a generic noun, *śakti* means energy or female potency; as a proper noun, Śakti is the feminine animating principle of the universe, which takes form as various goddesses and which is paired with Śiva.

Śambhu: The Origin of Happiness; a name for Śiva.

Śaṅkara: One of the most common epithets for Śiva.

Śaṅkarā: Wife of Śaṅkara; Kālī or Umā.

Śāradā Debī: Rāmkṛṣṇa's wife (1853–1920), who shared in his *sādhana* and helped him care for his disciples at the Daksinesvar temple.

sari: A cloth worn by Indian women, with one end wrapped and pleated around the waist to form an ankle-length skirt and the other draped across the midriff and over one shoulder. Often the top end of the sari is used to cover the head in modesty.

Satī: Śiva's wife Pārvatī in a former birth as the daughter of Dakṣa, who kills herself in outrage to protest her father's insult to Śiva. Śiva's grief is assuaged when she promises him to be born again as his wife.

sattva, *rajas*, and *tamas*: See *guṇas*.

Śiva: Lit. the Auspicious One; the husband of Umā and Kālī; one of the three principal gods of the Hindu pantheon, primarily responsible for the destruction of the universe.

Śrīmanta: A merchant in the *Caṇḍīmaṅgalakāvya* to whom the Goddess Kamalekāminī or Caṇḍī appears in the midst of the ocean. Eventually, after a number of adventures in which she saves him from death, he publicizes her worship.

Śumbha and Niśumbha: The two demons whom Durgā kills at the climax of the third story of the "Devī-Māhātmya."

suṣumnā: The most important of the arteries (*nāḍīs*) of the subtle body, which runs up through the spinal cord and is the channel through which the *kuṇḍalinī* travels to meet her mate in the thousand-petaled lotus at the top of the head.

svādhiṣṭhāna: The second of the seven *cakras* in the subtle body, situated (in the male) between the anus and the penis.

Śyāmā: Black One, a synonym for Kālī.

Śyāmā-saṅgīta: Songs to Śyāmā, the Black Goddess Kālī; one of the two parts of the Śākta Padāvalī genre.

Tantra: A ritual and philosophical system probably current in eastern India at least by the tenth century C.E., into which the worship of Kālī was incorporated by the eleventh century. Tantra is based upon the following principles: that worldly things usually considered as obstacles to spiritual advancement need not be so, if properly understood and handled; that the human body is a microcosm of the spiritual universe; and that non-dual liberation can be experienced within the body by a series of internalized ritual and meditation prescriptions, often focused on experiencing and harnessing the divine energy within. *Kuṇḍalinī* yoga is one such Tantric practice.

Tantrasāra: A Tantric digest or compendium composed in the seventeenth century by the famed Tantric adept, Kṛṣṇānanda Āgambāgīś.

Tārā: Savior, She Who Takes Across (the sea of this world); an epithet for Kālī.

Tribeni: Lit. three streams; confluence of three rivers; the meeting place, in the subtle body, of the three *nāḍīs*—*iḍā*, *piṅgalā*, and *suṣumnā*—in the *ājñā cakra* between the eyebrows.

Tripurāri: The Enemy of Tripura, the demons' triple city; an epithet for Śiva.

Tripurā-Sundarī: The Beautiful Goddess of Triple Nature; an epithet for Kālī.

Umā: Another name for Pārvatī, Śiva's wife.

Umā-saṅgīta: Songs to Umā; the second half (along with Śyāmā-saṅgīta) of the Śākta Padāvalī literary genre.

Vaiṣṇava Padāvalī: Songs to Kṛṣṇa and Caitanya, composed in Bengal from the fifteenth century which provide the model—in style, imagery, and devotional orientation—for the later Śākta Padāvalī tradition.

vātsalya bhāva: The feeling of a cow for her calf, exemplified in the Vaiṣṇava context by Yaśodā's attitudes toward her son Kṛṣṇa, and in the Śākta context by Menakā's love for Umā.

Vedas: The ancient, sacred scripture of the Hindu religious tradition which, in the Goddess-centered poetry of this book, is often said to be inadequate to reveal the glories of Kālī and Umā.

vijayā: Songs sung on the ninth and tenth days of the Durgā Pūjā festivities to lament Umā's imminent departure from her parents' home. For Vijayā, see Jayā.

Viṣṇu: The god responsible for the maintenance of the universe; one of the three great deities of the Hindu tradition (together with Brahmā and Śiva).

viśuddha: The fifth *cakra*, located in the throat.

Vrindavan: The small town and its wooded environs where Kṛṣṇa sported with the cowherd women; a symbol of passion and earthly harmony.

yantras: Mystic diagrams, essential to Tantric ritual.

yogi: Ascetic, master of spiritual discipline.

zamindars: Owners of landed estates, mostly in western Bengal, who frequently adopted Durgā and Kālī as their clan deities and who patronized their worship through rituals, festivals, and devotional literature.

Discography

The following list is a representative sample of cassettes produced (mainly in Calcutta) since 1981. A cassette that contains a recording of one of the songs translated in this book is marked with an asterisk (⋆).

Āj Āgamanīr Ābāhane. Singer: Maheś Rañjan Som. Gathani 4745. 1989.

Āpan Hate Āpan: Bāṅglā Bhaktigīti. Singer: Dīpti Basu. Atlantis AND 026. 1994.

⋆ *Ār Kono Sādh Nāi Mā: Śyāmā Saṅgīt*. Singer: Śrīkumār Caṭṭopādhyāy. HMV FPHVS 843110. 1998.

Āy Mā Umā Āy: Āgamanī o Bijayār Gān. Singers: Abhayāpad Caṭṭopādhyāy and K. Mallik. HMV TPHV 842705. 1995.

Baraṣā Phurāye Gelo: Bhinna Bhinna Svāder Āgamanī Saṅgīt. Singer: Tārāpad Caṭṭopādhyāy. Super Master Voice B01/50. 1993.

Bhaktigīti. Singer: Hīrālāl Sarkhel. Hindusthan Records 1722–0087. 1982.

⋆ *Bhaktigīti*. Singer: Pānnālāl Bhaṭṭācārya. HMV SPHO 23033. 1983.

De Mā Śyāmā Āmāy Dekhā. Singers: Anurādhā Poyḍāl and Indrajīt. Super Cassettes Industries T Series SBNC 01/120. 1995.

⋆ *Ḍub de re man Kālī bale: Bhaktigīti*. Singer: Dhanañjay Bhaṭṭācārya. Hindusthan Records 2722–C375 (1989).

⋆ *Eto Gaynā Beṭī Kothāy Peli: Bhaktigīti*. Singer: Rāmkumār Caṭṭopādhyāy. Hindusthan Records 1722–C376. 1989.

⋆ *Hṛd Padme Padmāsane*. Singer: Śrīkumār Caṭṭopādhyāy. Beethoven Records 120. 1997.

Jagat Jananī Māgo. Singer: Anup Jāloṭā. Atlantis AND 091. 1995.

⋆ *Jāgo He Ei Nagarbāsī: Bhaktigīti*. Singer: Amar Pāl. HMV TPHVS 28116. 1987.

Jāgo Jāgo Durgā. Singers: Śekhar and Kalyāṇī. Gathani 4801. 1989.

⋆ *Kājī Najruler Abismaraṇīya Śyāmā Saṅgīt (Devotional Songs of Kazi Najrul)*. Singers: Pānnālāl Bhaṭṭācārya, Mṛṇālkānti Ghoṣ, Anup Ghoṣāl, Añjali Mukhopādhyāy, Mānabendra Mukhopādhyāy, and Sandhyā Mukhopādhyāy. HMV TPHV 28030. 1988.

Kālī Kalpataru. Singer: Rāmkumār Caṭṭopādhyāy. HMV STHVS 24162. 1989.

Kālī Kīrtan. Singers: Āndul Kālī-Kīrtan Samiti. Madhuri Musicals M-101/2/-96. 1996.

⋆ *Kālo Meyer Pāyer Talāy: Bāṅglā Bhaktigīti*. Singer: Mṛṇālkānti Ghoṣ. HMV STHV 24103. 1988.

Kathāmṛter Citrapaṭe. Singer: Maheś Rañjan Som. HMV SPHOS 23108. 1989.

⋆ *Kicchu Nāi Saṃsārer Mājhe: Śyāmā Saṅgīt*. Singer: Śrīkumār Caṭṭopādhyāy. CBS Inc. 1991.

Mā Āmār Mā. Singer: Mānnā De. Gathani 7870. 1998.

⋆ *Mā go Ānandamayī*. Singer: Ānurādhā Poḍyāl. Super Cassettes Industries. SNCD 01/295. 1994.

* *Mā Yār Ānandamayī*. Singer: Ajay Cakrabartī. HMV TPHVS 842165. 1993.
* *Man Calo Nija Niketane*. Singer: Anup Jāloṭā. Music India 4227 976. 1989.
* *Man re Kṛṣi Kāj Jāno Nā: Bāṅglā Chāyāchabir Bhaktimūlak Gān*. Singer: Dhanañjay Bhaṭṭācārya. HMV STHV 824299. 1984.

Mātṛ Sādhan. Singer: Amar Prasād Caṭṭopādhyāy. Gathani 4579. 1988.

* *Najrul Gīti*. Singer: Anup Ghoṣāl. 2 vols. Farida Electronics. N.d.

Premer Ṭhākur Śrī Rāmkṛṣṇa Gīti Ālekhya. Super Sound 188. N.d.

* *Rāmkṛṣṇāyaṇ*. HMV HTCS 02B 22802. 1982.
* *Rāmprasādī Bāṅglā Bhaktigīti*. Singer: Maheś Rañjan Som. HMV TPHVS 842532. 1994.
* *Rāṅgā Caraṇ*. Singer: Amṛk Singh Arorā. Gathani 7664. 1996.
* *Rāṅgā Jabā Ke Dilo Tor Pāye?* Singer: Rāmkumār Caṭṭopādhyāy. Hindusthan Records 1722–C170. N.d.

Sādhak Kabi Rāmprasād. Super Sound 002. N.d.

* *Sādhanā: Bhaktigīti Saṅkalan*. Singer: Anup Ghoṣāl. Anupama Audio Cassette Co. AAC 001. 1989.

Sādhanā o Bandanā. Singer: Rāmkumār Caṭṭopādhyāy. JMD Sounds Ltd. BD 0258. 1998.

Sādhanāy Ārādhanāy. Singer: Rāmkumār Caṭṭopādhyāy. Prasad Digit Audio PDA/B 0004. 1996.

Śaktirūpiṇī Mā. Singer: Anup Ghoṣāl. Sound Wing SWC 5005. 1998.

* *Sangitanjali*. Singer: Pandit Ajay Chakrabarty. Sagarika 31050. 1994.
* *Songs from the Kathamrita*. Singer: Mahesh Ranjan Som. 3 vols. Ramakrishna Mission Saradapitha. 1987.

Śrī Śrī Rāmkṛṣṇa Kathāmṛta. Singer: Rāmkumār Caṭṭopādhyāy. Hindusthan Records 1723–C178. N.d.

Śyāmā Nāme Lāglo Āgun: Śyāmā Saṅgīt. Singers: Amṛk Singh Arorā, Dhanañjay Bhaṭṭācārya, Amar Prasād Caṭṭopādhyāy, Rāmkumār Caṭṭopādhyāy, Śrīkumār Caṭṭopādhyāy, Svarāj Rāy, Hīrālāl Sarkhel, and Maheś Rañjan Som. 4 vols. Gathani 7410-7413. 1984.

Śyāmā Saṅgīt. Singer: Asitābh. Super Cassettes Industries T Series SBNC 01/12. 1988.

* *Śyāmā Saṅgīt*. Singer: Dhanañjay Bhaṭṭācārya. Gathani 04027. N.d.

Śyāmā Saṅgīt. Singers: Dhanañjay Bhaṭṭācārya, Pānnālāl Bhaṭṭācārya, and Svarāj Rāy. Gathani 04007. 1981.

* *Śyāmā Saṅgīt*. Singer: Pānnālāl Bhaṭṭācārya. HMV HTC 2739. 1981.
* *Śyāmā Saṅgīt*. Singer: Pānnālāl Bhaṭṭācārya. Indian Record Co. 2722-0045. 1981.
* *Śyāmā Saṅgīt*. Singer: Rāmkumār Caṭṭopādhyāy. EMI HTCS 02B 2597. 1985.

Śyāmā Saṅgīt. Singer: Svarāj Rāy. Gathani 4196. 1986.

* *Śyāmā Saṅgīt*. Singer: Maheś Rañjan Som. Gathani 4281. 1989.

Śyāmā Saṅgīt: Bhaktigīti. Singer: Hīrālāl Sarkhel. Gathani 4220. 1988.

Śyāmā Saṅgīt o Rāmprasādī. Singer: Bhabānī Dās. Megaphone JNLXC 1031. 1981.

* *Trinayanī: Śyāmā Saṅgīt*. Singer: Amṛk Singh Arorā. Gathani 7551 (1995).

Ye Phule Tomāy Añjali Dii. Singers: Pralubdha Kānti and Pratāp Nārāyaṇ. Indian Music Co. 01C X0310. N.d.

Index of Poems by Author and First Line (English)

Index of Poems by Author and First Line (Bengali)